SAINT CATHERINE OF SIENNE

Mons. LODOVICO FERRETTI o.p.

SAINT CATHERINE
OF SIENA

EDIZIONI CANTAGALLI

Traduzione dall'italiano di Sonia di Centa

Imprimatur:
† Gaetano Bonicelli
Arcivescovo Metropolita
Sienne, 8 luglio 1996

Stampato da Edizioni Cantagallli s.r.l.
Siena, giugno 2011
via Massetana Romana, 12 - Tel. 0577/42102 Fax 45363

CONTENTS

SAINT CATHERINE

On the Feast of the Annunciation, which in that year, 1347, coincided with Palm Sunday, twin girls were born to Giacomo Benincasa, a dyer of the Fontebranda section of the Goose district in Siena, and his wife Lappa di Nuccio Piangenti. These two little girls, Giovanna and Catherine, joined an already rather large family of 22 other brothers and sisters: Giovanna died, however, immediately after her baptism, while Catherine survived in order to love and suffer for the next thirty-three years.

The Benincasa family, well-known for its Christian faith and piety, was bound by a deep and reverent affection to the Dominican Fathers of Camporegio, and their imposing church which still dominates the hill overlooking Fontebranda and affords an excellent view of the entire city, was assiduosly frequented by all its members. Catherine's family, unusually large even by the standards of the late middle ages including in-laws and cousins, was permeated naturally, by the teachings of Christianity thanks above all to Giacomo, a gentle, patient soul, and Lapa, a much more nervous even querellous type of person. They were honest hard-working parents thought and they provided for their children not only the material necessities of life, but also an atmospheare of stability and peace. When Catherine was only a year old the Black Death had already begun its gruesome work of eliminating one third of Europe's population; among those so cruelly eliminated were the parents of a ten-year old boy named Tommaso della Fonte who, shortly afterwards was adopted by the Benincasa family thanks to the efforts of one of Catherine's elder sisters, Niccoluccia, whose husband, Palmiere della Fonte, was the boy's uncle. Little Tommaso had already felt a strong attraction towards the Dominican Order an he enjoyed learning about its brief, but fascinating history and talking about it to everyone in his new family. As Catherine was growing up, she was especially impressed by Tommaso's stories, even to the point of piously kissing the footprints of any Dominican priest who happened to pass in front of her house.

Catherine was evidently a very devout little girl and when she was about six years of age the most decisive event of her whole life occurred. One day, as she was walking with one of her brothers, Stefano – perhaps they were returning home on having completed an errand for their mother – Catherine stopped and looked up at the majestic Church of Saint Dominic dominating the hill of Camporegio and at that very instant had a vision of Jesus Christ seated on a splendid throne dressed and crowed as a pope, and flanked by the Apostles, Peter, Paul and John. Catherine remained immovable for what seemed to be a very long time and felt an inexpressible joy when Jesus smiled and, raising his right hand, blessed her. Stefano, who had continued walking all this time, noticed Catherine's absence, waited a few seconds for her to emerge from her trance and then yelled to her impatiently. At that moment her attention snapped and she lowered her eyes in order to see where her brother was, but when she looked up at the church again, the vision had vanished. Catherine immediately felt a sharp pang of sorrow and burst into childish tears. Shortly after this episode, her adopted brother Tommaso decided to become a Dominican and entered the novitiate in the Priory of San Domenico and inspired by his example and by the stories she had heard from his lips about the Holy Martyrs, the virgins and the fathers of the desert, Catherine also decided that she wanted to go to the desert in order to love and serve God. Why should she not, she reasoned accept the evangelical inviation to abandon everything – father, mother brothers, sisters, home – and go to live in a cave, the better to be alone with God and talk to Him? Even though she had never before dared to wander beyond the city walls, Catherine resolved to carry out her intention. One morning, having supplied herself with a piece of bread she quietly slipped out of the house and walked towards the gate of San Sano on the outskirts of Siena. Thinking to find a cave of the good within short distance, she boldly continued walking for a good while until she finally saw some of them dotting the hills of the surrounding countryside; she chose one, entered it, knelt down and began praying with all the arbour of her infant spirit. Catherine spent almost the entire day in this precocious ecstasy until the bells of San Domenico announced the approach of evening. She returned to her senses and, with a childlike intuition of God's will, retraced her steps back to the gate of San Sano and arrived safely home without arousing the suspicion of the others who presumed that she had simply paid an unusually long visit to one of her elder married sisters. Catherine understood – or thought she did – what God wanted of her: to leave the world behind, live in solitude and listen to

9

him speaking to her in the depths of her heart. From that moment on, Catherine began to fell a hunger and a thirst for the things of Heaven and, gradually, to weigh the value of earthly joys, human affections and her own life in relation to the Eternal Goodness that had been revealed to her. She realised that only God was the Highest Good and that everything else was utterly empty and insignificant compared to Him; and this elementary truth became so clear and fixed in her mind that, raising herself above all wordly concerns she understood that only God could fill her heart and make her happy. Catherine thus felt transformed and sharply separated in her thoughts, desires and aspirations from everyone else in her own family who were so intent on pursuing the things of this life and hoping to find happiness in them. She knew that only God in His infinite Goodness was worthy of all her love and felt acute anguish in the fact that her little heart was incapable of containing Him. Catherine's prayers had nothing in common with those which other small children habitually recited; they really welled up from her mind and heart and even her body seemed to participate in the fervour of her soul.

Notwithstanding her tender age, Catherine knew that she prayed best when she was alone. During these moments of solitude she perceived more clearly the voice of God speaking to her an she even tried to find little hideouts all around the house where she could prolongue her devotions. She would conceal herself for hours in these beloved retreats conversing with the Lord who flooded her soul with light, grace and joy.

All these spiritual activities did not distract her, though, from normal life. Catherine was cheerful and courteous with her brothers and sisters, and she always showed particular respect and affection towards her parents and, even though she had formed a rather peculiar habit of reciting the Hail Mary on her knees for every step of the stairs, she would immediately bounce to her feet and fly up and down those same stairs in obedience to the slightest request from her siblings or parents.

There was only one thing she could not habituate herself to: the hearty nourishing meals enjoyed so much by the others. The amount of food their mother prepared seemed excessive to Catherine; she preferred to subsist on bread and a few herbs, and she never drank wine. Whenever she was given meat, she slipped it into Stefano's plate and, in this way, Catherine trained herself to eat what was only strictly necessary in order to obtain complete self-mastery and grew in her desire to live in union with God.

MOTHER LAPA

Catherine's mother was a restless, keen-witted, no-nonsense woman who did not see much to admire in the way of life her small daughter was creating for herself. Lapa felt an especial affection for Catherine, the only one of her numerous brood she had been able to breast feed because of her continual pregnancies, and she had the satisfaction of seeing her become a robust, attractive child; but she also looked with a wary eye on all those long prayers, retreats, abstinences, vigils, and certain other mortifications that Catherine was no able to keep secret and which began to visibly weaken her. And she became quite alarmed when she discovered that her favourite daughter had made a habit of leaving her bed almost every night in order to sleep on the rough tiles of the floor. Lapa shrewdly concluded that Catherine needed a husband and that the duties of married life would be the most efficient means of distracting her from all those incomprehensible austerities. In the late middle ages, Sienese city life was (as it still is today) marked by many popular civil festivities which were considered as an excellent occasions by mothers or elder sister for presenting their young, pretty, well dressed marriageable girls to public gaze. Lapa found a prompt and able ally in her married daughter Bonaventura, of whom Catherine was very fond, and who finally convinced her younger sister to pay more attention to her appearance and to make herself more attractive like most girls of the time (as now) were wont to do. Catherine at first resisted their suggestions but finally, to avoid further arguments, gave in to their importunities; she had already completed her fifteenth year of age, was rather pretty and radiated a certain graciousness and innocence which could easily have won her a husband. She had already made, however, some years previously, a vow of absolute virginity to God and she showed herself in public just a few times only in order to pacify her mother and sister while maintaining always her firm intention not to be contaminated by worldly vanities. In that same year, 1362, Bonaventura died during childbirth and Catherine, seized by sharp pains of remorse for having followed her advice about making herself more physically attractive, renounced forever all such earthly concerns and pleasures, and resolved to return to her former penitent way of life. Catherine had agreed to make her debut in Siena social life only to please her sister and, even though her confessor, the learned Raymond di Capua, assured her later on that Bonaventura's death was not her fault, she never forgot the unhappy episode nor forgave herself for what she considered to be a grave sin on her part. Catherine's conscience may have been a bit too delicate and even laughable compared to our hard bitten twentieth-century ones, but it was undoubtedly more admirable. Tommaso della Fonte, meanwhile had already been ordained a priest in the Dominican Order and, thanks to his precocious reputation for sanctity, Catherine had chosen him to be her spiritual director. Giacomo and Lapa were quite pleased with this development, thinking that Tommaso was just the man to prevail upon their daughter to abandon her abnormal religious practices; and he accepted the challenge. Catherine disclosed to him the secrets of her soul, above all the absolute resolution that Jesus would be the only love of her life. She had already given her entire heart to Him and had no more love to spare for a merely human husband. Catherine spoke with such fervour and certitude that Tommaso not only ceased to doubt her, but told her that if her decision was really so radical and irrevocable, to take a pair of scissors and without wasting any more time cut off totally, or almost, her lovely long-flowing hair. So she did it; and, in order to hide her rather clumsy barbering efforts, began going around with a white veil on her head. When Lapa discovered her daughter's new unusual hairdo, she was for a moment – but only for one moment assuredly – speechless with shock before reacting with shrieks of rage and pain against Catherine in front of the entire family; only Giacomo managed to keep a cool head and not to rashly condemn his insubordinate daughter. An unassuming, easy-going man in all situations, Giacomo was unable to restrain his wife from punishing Catherine physically, even acquiescing in her decision to deprive Catherine of her own little bedroom and forcing her to share one with her brother Stefano. Thanks to this rough experience Catherine learned one of the great truths of the Christian life: even when it is not possible to live in external solitude, one can always retire into oneself, or more precisely, into the interior cell of the heart. And one can live in this latter solitude at all rimes and in all places, even in the thick of routine duties and the press of human transactions, listening to God's voice and working with Him for the salvation of souls. Catherine persevered in her prayers while sharing Stefano's bedroom without complaining

14

about the harsh treatment she was receiving and, one day, the Lord decided to confirm her progress in sanctity in a special way. One morning, as Catherine was alone in the room praying on her knees, Giacomo was passing by, and, stopping for a moment, he peered at her through a crack in the wooden door and saw a snow-white dove nestled upon her head. He immediately called for Lapa, but by the time she arrived the dove had disappeared. From that day on, Catherine's parents began to understand that she was destined for higher things than the world could offer and that God was guiding her according to His own designs. It was useless to fight against Him.

Catherine thus, got her old room back, bare and unattractive as it was, but dear to her, and continued her prayers and penitences. Lapa, however had not completely surrendered and she still tried to think of other ways to distract her daughter from her spiritual fixations. She conceived the idea of taking Catherine to some hot springs at Vignone, a small town in the Tuscan countryside of Val d'Orcia, which were famous for their health-restoring waters. Catherine, upon obtaining permission to bathe alone, turned the cure into a torture by positioning herself right under the spray of boiling hot water and, with astonishing resistance, survived the treatment by thinking of the pains of Purgatory. The desire to suffer had become second nature to her and she dreamt of offering her whole life as a holocaust of love to God. Upon returning home Catherine heard about the existence of the Third Order of Penance which the great Founder of the Dominican Order, Saint Dominic, had created with the noble intention of giving lay people the opportunity of collaborating in the work of spreading the faith, defending the rights of the Church and sanctifying themselves in the process. A small group of these devoted men and women already existed in Siena and, among them was a good number of widows who, under the direction of one of the Dominican Fathers led an almost totally cloistered life, each in own home. The people of Siena called them the Mantellate because they all wore a black "mantello" or cape over a simple tunic fastened tightly to their bodies by a black leather belt and their religious garb was topped with a white veil upon their heads. These pious ladies were not nuns in the modern sense of the word, nor were they juridically tied to the Dominican Order by the vows of poverty, chastity and obedience or by any particular monastic rule. They assiduously frequented the Church of San Domenico for their religious practices usually in the so-called Chapel of the Vaults, famous today thanks to Saint Catherine. There was, however, only one obstacle in the way of Catherine's desire to join this congregation; she was too young, still only a teen-ager. And, thought Catherine begged her mother to intercede on her behalf with the Prioress, Lapa was quite happy to discover that such an impediment existed and absolutely delighted when the Prioress explicitly declared that her daughter was too young and pretty to join their group. Divine providence, however had – as usual – an ace up Its sleeve, and facilitated Catherine's entry into the Mantellate by allowing her to come down with smallpox. Her whole body was ravaged with blisters and consumed with a burning fever and she warned an anxious Lapa that she would not recover unless she could join the Mantellate. The Prioress agreed to visit Catherine at her home with some of the other sisters and they were so favourably impressed by Catherine's angelic words and demeanour that even though her girlish beauty returned after the bout with disease, her virtues were judged to be solid enough for admittance to the Mantellate. So Catherine entered the Third Order of Saint Dominic and became during her brief life its greatest member and honour, personifying and extending its activities for the good of souls, the support of the weak, the comfort of the helpless and the defence of the Church. And those same sisters who once hesitated to welcome her into their group soon learned to love and revere her as Mother and Guide. But for the moment, nobody could or would have predicted that God had planned such an illustrious career for this humble, illiterate girl. Catherine herself was content to know her place in this new family and, in the meantime, her only preoccupation was to nourish the love for God she felt in her heart. For the next three years she lived in rigorous retirement and almost continuous silence, stepping outside her house only when it was necessary to go up to San Domenico and participate at Mass and the Divine Office, which she listened attentively to the other Mantellate recite since she didn't know how to read, and to receive spiritual direction from her confessor, Tommaso della Fonte. While at home, she lived in her austere little room taking just enough food and drink to survive, conversing familiarly with her Lord, the blessed Virgin and the angels and saints and, gradually, winning the respect and admiration of everyone. Only God, of course, knew what was happening in Catherine's soul during the long nights she passed in solitude watching and praying until the bells of San Domenico summoned the friars to their pre-dawn devotions. And as the silence to the night was being so rudely interrupted by the tolling of those bells, Catherine used to say: "Behold, O Lord, your servants, my brothers, have been sleeping until now and I have remained awake in you Presence. Shortly, they shall praise your name: protect them and increase your grace in them and grant me now a little sleep". Then, she dropped off the once but never, literally, for more than a couple of hours. She would wake up to greet the dawn of a new day with praises of God on her lips.

BRIDE OF CHRIST

The good Lord especially loves those souls who prefer to consecrate their hearts and their lives to Him in love rather than to earthly pleasures and He uses such people, purified and sanctified by His grace, as precious instruments to extend the benefits of salvation to all mankind. These people in general and, holy women in particular, become intimate associates in the work of redemption and the Redeemer Himself calls them His brides. Their lamps are always shining brightly thanks to the oil of faith, hope and charity and the gospel of Matthew shows their readiness to respond to the invitation to their spouse. Among all the elected souls in the history of Christianity, Catherine certainly earned the right to be called the Bride of Christ more, perhaps, than any other woman. Her first and most famous biographer, Raymond of Capua, enjoyed recounting the different ways in which Christ visibly confirmed Catherine's supernatural mission: the wedding ring, the crown of thorns, the exchange of hearts and the wound in her hands, feet and side. In 1367, on the last Thursday before Lent, while all Siena was in the midst of its usual merry-making, Catherine was alone at home praying more intensely than ever. The world no longer existed for her, she felt completely separated from other people and had no desire to see or share their trivial and even sinful pursuit. She felt so close to God and her heart was so brim-full with His love that other things had simply ceased to count. Catherine was already entering the highest stages of contemplation in which she heard the Lord speaking to her the words He had spoken to the ancient Israelites through the prophet Hosea "I will betroth you in faithfulness". Upon hearing these words Catherine experienced in the depths of her soul the first sublime episode of her mystical life. She saw the Lord Jesus Himself, holding in His hand a brilliant golden ring, accompanied by the blessed Virgin Mary, Saint John the Evangelist, Saint Paul, Saint Dominic and David who was sweetly playing a harp. Our Lady then took Catherine's hand and placed it in that of her Divine Son as He slipped the wedding ring on Catherine's finger, exhorting her with heavenly words to work courageously for the glory of God, armed with the faith. When the vision vanished, Catherine knew that she had reached the end of her retired life. She was twenty years old and after having tasted the joys of the purely contemplative life, felt irresistably called to the active apostolic life, not knowing exactly, however, where or how to begin. But she trusted fully in God to guide her and, in order to make Catherine understand that she must go out into the world, He no longer manifested Himself to Her in her tiny room, but outside the door commanding her to come out. Even the habit she wore proclaimed her to be the daughter of an Order called to action and apostolic work for the salvation of souls and the honour of being the bride of Christ stimulated her to work for the glory of her Spouse and inflame the entire world with His love.

Catherine's first field of action was, obviously her own home. God had given her the power to speak in His name and she used it well when she convinced two nieces, the daughter of her sister-in-law Lisa, who was also a member of the Mantellate in San Dominic, to embrace the religious life; the two little girls listened to the voice of the Lord, and thanks to Catherine became cloistered nuns at the Convent in Montepulciano, forty-four miles southeast of Siena by rail, already famous because of the holy Dominican virgin, Saint Agnes, who had lived there fifty years before Catherine's birth. All the members of her family, Lapa a bit less than the others, now listened to Catherine's words with respect, even awe; particularly when those words, normally so sweet and humble, became fiery and imperious in asserting the honour of God and threatening woe to anyone who tried to oppose them. Even the good Friars of San Domenico venerated by Catherine as though angels from heaven, sometimes hesitated to openly contradict the dyer's daughter. Quite often they stumbled upon her as she was praying in ecstasy in their church and observed her closely; her face was pale, her eyes full of tears, a celestial radiance seemed to emanate from her whole person. And everyone, priests, religious and lay people testified that Catherine with her words and deeds always encouraged them to lead holier lives. Catherine showered all her love on her vast spiritual family, especially the poor, who were her dearest friends; real, visible personifications in flesh and blood of Jesus who said "Whatever you did for the least of my brothers, you did for me". And once, Christ Himself really appeared to her as a poor man begging to be fed and clothed. After having received permission from her parents to succour the needy with some of their household goods, Catherine's generosity knew no limits. She would often go to the local hospital, just across the street facing the Cathedral, appearing like an angel of mercy to the sick, the hungry, and tired pilgrims. And none of the other members of Mantellate of San Domenico who served as nurses in the hospital could hold a candle to Catherine when it came to consoling the patients in their material and spiritual necessities. "Nobody has ever spoken to us like this woman" they used to declare; and just seeing her and listening to her brought them much inner tranquillity. Catherine even volunteered to take care of lepers and showed no fear of contracting their highly contagious, piteous disease. The city fathers had established a special house for them well outside the walls called Saint Lazzarus, a good half hour walk from Fontebranda and Catherine went to visit them almost every day. And if she met any who refused her charitable ministrations she doubled her visits and efforts to overcome their loneliness and bitterness of heart and, often, with her prayers obtain a complete cure in body and mind for them. Even the gaols opened their doors to Catherine. She entered and exited them quite freely bringing the soothing power of her words to alleviate the miserable existence of the inmates, many of whom were perfectly innocent of any serious wrongdoing and were in prison only because they had happened to be on the losing side in the frequent and unedifying political struggles of the day. Catherine's brief presence filled their unhappy lives with light and many of them followed her exhortations to bear their misfortunes with patience and hope and many, perhaps for the first time in their lives acquired some real peace of soul as they more or less cooperated with God's grace. Catherine's words were particularly efficacious when it came to advising patients suffering from terminal disease to look realistically at their situation and prepare for the solemn moment of death and, as usual, her admonitions penetrated not only the ears but also the hearts of even the most unpromising candidates, particularly the notorious criminal Andrea dei Bellanti whom she accompanied to the gallows after he had repented and confessed his sins.

CATHERINE'S FATHER

Rising loftily above the steep narrow road on Via del Costone which leads from the opposite side of Siena into Fontebranda district, the impressive church of Saint Dominic towers high above the valley like some austere impregnable fortress crowning the hill of Camporegio. This name, which means "the regal field" or "the King's camp" was probably given to the hill when Henry, King of the Romans, used it as his base of operations during the siege he led against Siena in 1186. The construction of Saint Dominic's was begun in 1225 and completed in 1262 but it consisted only of the nave or vertical part; the transept, or horizontal part, was begun a few years later, and in order to support its weight an elegant crypt was at first called the "Church of the Deceased", because many members of noble families and of the Third Order, along with other friends and benefactors of the Dominican Fathers, often asked to be buried within its hallowed walls; and the good Fathers, just as often granted their permission for the fulfilment of these pious requests and prayed daily for the eternal rest of all those hopeful souls. On august 22, 1368 Catherine's father died and the Dominicans most willingly accorded him an honourable resting place in their crypt, and, shortly afterwards they reserved a special burial vault for the entire Benincasa family. Many relatives and acquaintances joined in the funeral procession from Fontebranda to Camporegio, trying to console poor Lapa who was totally distraught with grief. Only Catherine managed to maintain internally and externally a certain composure and tranquillity. She alone had prepared her father's corpse for the coffin and arranged all the necessary details for the funeral ceremony and without wasting a single tear, even helped the graveyard diggers as they lowered Giacomo into the ground. To those who were surprised and reproachful towards Catherine for her apparent coldness and lack of filial piety, she replied: "May it please the Lord to send all of us a similar death!". She had assisted her father during his last illness, had reminded him that the solemn moment of death was nearing closer, had prayed for his eternal salvation as he humbly resigned himself to the divine will and had watched him die in peace. Catherine never doubted for a moment that he had gone straight to heaven and tried to communicate to the members of her family this comforting conviction. Catherine interceded for the father's salvation with sighs, prayers and tears and obtained it on one condition; her heavenly Spouse made her bear the pains that would have been inflicted on Giacomo in Purgatory in expiation for his sins. The good Lord granted Catherine's desires because her one and only preoccupation during her life, as becomes a true Dominican, was the salvation of souls and the supernatural consolation she experienced in knowing that her father was enjoying the happiness of heaven allowed her to take such an apparently unemotional view of his death. Even the above-mentioned pains that she lovingly endured for the rest of her life were sweet to Catherine and useful for the purification of her own soul. All the members of the Benincasa Family eventually came to rest in that special burial vault in the crypt of Saint Dominic and, of course, an honoured place was reserved for Lapa next to her beloved husband. In 1619 the remains of the entire family were transferred to the upper church under the marble altar of the little chapel which contains that priceless treasure of Siena, the Sacred Head of Saint Catherine.

THE TWO CROWNS

There were, are, and always will be people who find everything laughable, who scorn what they cannot comprehend, who attempt to measure all things according to their own limited viewpoints and during her short life Catherine was one of the favourite targets of the scoffers. They considered her way of life to be suitable only for a madwoman and her mystical visions and experiences as the fruit of an overheated imagination; and the fame that already surrounded her name everywhere was looked upon simply as the effect of a subtle cleverness or a studied vainglory. The marvelous wonders that Divine Love produced in Catherine's soul, making her feel as if it had been shot forth from her body into eternity, were misunderstood and judged maliciously; and her followers who witnessed these extraordinary events were taken for dreamers or dupes. Other people, who were more generously inclined, concluded that Catherine's tenor of life was simply exaggerated, not very helpful for growth in the virtues, especially prudence and the duty of keeping oneself in reasonably good health, temperance; and they openly abhored that continuous privation of food and sleep, which was causing Catherine such evident pain and taking heavy toll on the robust constitution nature had endowed her with. As her fame spread from her Fontebranda neighbourhood over all Siena, Catherine must have heard about the uncharitable things her detractors were saying about her. She, however, took a typically charitable attitude towards her enemies, calling them friends and benefactors. My defects are so numerous, she used to say, they haven't even begun to list them all. Not that the doubts and unjustified suspicions which many people entertained did not cause Catherine great inward pain, particularly when they existed in the minds of priests and religious consecrated to God. But rather than judge them harshly, Catherine took advantage of their murmurings to ruthlessly examine her own character just in case there was a grain of truth in what her critics said. She thus felt even more inspired to humble herself and grow in perfection. After every self-examination she experienced a great peace of soul and she resolved to persevere in doing all the good that God called her to do. And, one day, her celestial Spouse gave her visible sign of His infinite predilection for her. He appeared to Catherine holding in His sacred hands two crowns: one was made of pure gold studded with precious brilliant jewels, the other was made of hard piercing thorns. Jesus spoke saying: "Take the one you prefer". And Catherine, without hesitating for an instant, chose the crown of thorns. The choice simply confirmed what she already understood; that she must bravely bear acute sufferings during this life, especially when they consisted of the above-mentioned cruel accusations, murmurings, suspicions and condemnations which were constantly launched against her way of life. And when Catherine discovered that all these things had reached the ears of the Master-General of the Dominician Order, Father Elia da Tolouse, she sent him the following note: "This is my glory, that others may speak evilly of me for the rest of my life. This is what I desire. I do not feel sorry for myself, but for them". By lovingly and patiently wearing the crown of thorns, Catherine won the right to wear the crown of gold and jewels for all eternity.

During this time Catherine's soul was undergoing a continual process of transformation that rendered it holier and lifted it above all the worries and commotions of earthly life. Whoever attentively observed her could not fail to notice that she was by now totally dominated and led by a superior will or divine grace which without destroying her rich natural talents, brought them to the peak of their perfection in her looks, in her word, in her exterior actions, in her whole life. Affable towards everybody, but maintaining a certain independence in her relationships, Catherine gradually acquired a self-possession and an imperturbability that quite astonished many who came into contact with her. She no longer looked at men, women, and life itself from a merely human viewpoint. This mysterious process of spiritual transformation reached its supreme consummation in July 1370 when Catherine had vision of Jesus, Who, placing His hands in her chest, extracted her heart of flesh and replaced it with His own Heart aflame with Divine Love, which burned away all the dross of Catherine's old nature and at the same time, purified her and changed her into a completely new creature. She immediately recognized with even greater clearness what her mission was; to save souls at any cost. But she had to seek them out, even leave her native city and go wherever God called her, ignoring all other voices. It was really as if God Himself whispered words to her ears, words so full of flaming love that they could have proceeded only from Him. As a group of loyal, devoted friends, men and women, began to form itself around her, Catherine used them almost as personal secretaries in order to extend her message outside the confines of Siena. They looked upon her as and began to call her their mother and teacher and Catherine began dictating her first letters "in the name of Christ Crucified and sweet Mary"; these letters were essentially invitations to conversion, exhortations to strive for greater sanctity, trenchant rebukes to people of all ranks who gloried in their vices. And while condemning the wicked acts of others and inciting them to perform the opposite works of goodness, Catherine's humility and genuine self-forgetfulness shone in the vibrant phrases she used in order to wake up the spirituality asleep, arouse their consciences, and frighten the evildoers. The vigorous intelligence that nature had given her and that the light of truth always so well illuminated, the tender heart always open to all the refinements of love and, thanks to the grace of God, able to embrace great and noble desires, are all revealed in the many letters Catherine dictated to her disciples and sent to men and women high and low, in all walks of life. All her letters are amazing feats of literacy, worthy of the most accomplished correspondents of any time or place, especially when one remembers that Catherine was a typically unschooled girl who had not yet learned to read and write. She acquired her literary talents directly from the Lord Himself and she exploited them to the full, tirelessly urging her readers to cultivate the virtues of love, peacefulness, generosity towards neighbours, absolute trust in God and sweet suffering with Christ. Catherine's missives display a masterly and harmonious blend of urbanity, eloquence, strength, and humility; intransigent with herself, but clement towards others, she invariably blamed herself when the others failed to live up to her high standards of Christian morality and apostolic work. She wrote, literally, to everyone: the near and the far, the poor and the rich, the low and the powerful, not excluding kings and popes and, especially towards folks in these last two categories she could use frighteningly energetic language. This epistolary apostolate of the virgin of Siena lasted for more than ten years and the brilliance and intensity of its flame was extinguished only at the instant Catherine died. But this is not true; thanks to the loving efforts of her disciples the spiritual motherhood of Catherine displayed in her letters has lasted and produced fruits of holiness for more than six centuries. Her letters are a priceless and essential component of the spiritual and intellectual heritage of humanity, required reading for anyone who wishes not only to understand Catherine's message in a purely theoretical way, but to be purified and sanctified by it and, thus, reach eternal salvation.

THE PLAGUE

Catherine was born right at the beginning of the infamous Black Death, which according to the best historians wiped out one-third of Europe's population; a similar plague that broke out in 1374 was less murderous, but nevertheless quite frightful. Like its more merciless predecessor it was no respecter of persons: the young and the old, the strong and the weak, the high and the low were all unwilling victims of the unwelcome and devastating visitation. Once a person was struck, death was only a matter of a few hours. In Catherine's own family eleven members were cruelly cut down by the plague's scythe: two brothers, one sister and eight among her nieces and nephews. And finding herself in the midst of such atrocious suffering, Catherine rose to the occasion. She rallied the other Mantellate around her and they did their best to console the sick and the dying. A certain Matthew Cenni, the head of the Hospital of Mercy gave Catherine a hand in these charitable works until he was brought down by the horrible disease and forced to take to his bed; when Catherine went to visit him she cried out: "Matthew, Matthew, this is no time to be lazy". And he immediately arose, completely healed. Many people who had fallen into total despair because of the miserable situation gave themselves unreservedly to the moment, snatching at even the basest fleeting pleasures to make their lives more tolerable; but when Catherine fired her rebukes like arrows at them, they repented and began to think more seriously about this life and the next. Blessed Raymond of Capua, fra Barthlomew Dominici and the hermit Fra Santi were Catherine's usual companions as they trudged up and down the sometimes torturous, winding, narrow streets of hilly Siena, entering the most lurid tenements and the overcrowded hospitals in order to at least save the souls of those whose bodies were beyond repair. Catherine's white habit alone was a joyous vision for her fellow-citizens who were desolated by the trouble of the times and she lavished on them her expertise in the art of spiritual consolation. In such moments she wielded a truly supernatural power conferred by God and many by her touch and her words were restored to perfect health. The plague eventually ceased; and Catherine, who had managed to remain uncontaminated during its entire course fell gravely ill. Her only desire was to leave this world and fly straight to heaven, but Our Lady appeared to her and showed her the many, many souls whose salvation depended upon her and Catherine realized that her work had only just begun.

AT MONTEPULCIANO

In the autumn of 1374 Catherine conceived an un-alterable desire to visit the hill-town of Montepulciano, less than fifty miles south of Siena, where the glorious Dominican Saint Agnes had died in 1317, leaving her nuns a treasury of edifying memories and an attractive example of heroic virtues. The fame of her sanctity and news of the miracles which took place through con-tact with her sacred corpse spread quickly throughout the whole Tuscan region; when Agnes died even the small children ran up and down the streets of the town crying: "The Saint is dead!". Her blessed body which is still incorrupt, had been left by the other nuns in their church for public veneration and fifty-seven years later it was still resting on the same catafalque, sur-rounded by golden votive offerings and its head was covered with a simple white drape. Catherine went to Montepulciano with two other Mantellate and, the fol-lowing day, Fra Tommaso della Fonte arrived there in the company of Blessed Raymond of Capua who had already lived at the monastery as the nuns' confessor for three years and had been recently nominated as their direct Superior by the Dominican Order. When they reached the convent the nuns lost no time in telling them about a charming wonder that had oc-curred on the previous day: Catherine had bowed low in order to affectionately and reverently kiss one of Agnes' feet and, at that very instant, the latter courte-ously raised her foot and met the former's lips in mid air! Catherine visited the monastery in Montepulciano many other times during her life: the second visit was made in the company of the two nieces who became nuns there. They were the daughters of her brother, Bartholomew, and their mother, Lisa, accompanied them on that important day. On this visit Catherine did almost the same thing as on the first one: she bowed low to venerate Agnes, placing her head next to that of the Saint and prayed intensely for a few minutes, then she raised her head and said to the onlookers: "Do you not see the gift that the Lord has sent you from heaven?". As Catherine was pronouncing the last word, the bystanders looked up and beheld a light rain of dew falling all around them. Catherine was always generous towards the sisters in Montepulciano; she did her best to sustain them in their material necessities, especially when their monastery fell upon hard times, and she wrote some lovely letters to her nieces, full of Christian wisdom. She urged them to live like true daughters of Saint Agnes and to imitate, most of all, that humility which had gained such great glory for her. To a certain Sister Eugenia who from her tenderest years had faithfully preserved the fresh flower of her baptismal innocence for Jesus, Catherine wrote advising her to keep in mind and to follow "the way" of their glorious Saint and to dedicate herself to prayer, solitude and union with God. The Lord Himself had already revealed to Catherine that she would attain the same grade of glory in paradise as Saint Agnes and that they would be inseparable companions for all eternity. This is the only happiness worth striving for, which Jesus offers to His loyal disciples, a happiness that will always seem incomprehensible to those who give their hearts to the riches, honours and pleasures of this world.

BLESSED RAYMOND DELLE VIGNE

While Catherine was ministering at the bedside of Matthew Cenni as he hovered between life and death, she met for the first time the saintly Dominican priest Raymond of Capua who came from a noble family descended from a certain Pier della Vigne, chancellor of the Holy Roman Emperor Frederick II. Catherine had glimpsed him more than once in the Church of Saint Dominic as he went about his pastoral duties in the company of Fra Tommaso della Fonte and Fra Bartholomew Dominici; it just so happened that she was seeking someone of his moral and intellectual stature to be her confessor and spiritual director, and after having asked Our Lady in prayer for guidance in the matter, chose him. Blessed Raymond was at that moment forty-seven years old and, as we have seen had already been living in Montepulciano as the official confessor of the Dominican nuns there. Catherine made a wise decision in entrusting her soul to Raymond. He greatly assisted her in those works of charity she performed during the plague of 1374 and he was her travelling companion and primary collaborator in her efforts to convince Pope Gregory XI to leave Avignon and return to Rome. Raymond, for his part, was a highly intelligent man who immediately recognized what was in front of him; the person he was dealing with was such an extraordinary vessel of grace that he gladly humbled himself before her and considered himself to be her most unworthy disciple. Even though he was older than she, he entrusted himself to her as to a most tender mother and whenever she spoke to him about the mysteries of the faith, of grace, of the joys that God grants to His elect on earth and in heaven, he, undoubtedly found in her a most enlightening teacher. Catherine was an almost inexhaustable source of comfort for Raymond during their brief partnership. She healed him of his various physical illnesses and strengthened him in his spiritual trials, stimulating him by her own example to persevere in scaling the heights of Christian perfection. The letters Catherine wrote show how delicately she tried to guide him and how tactfully she humbled herself before him, asking his pardon for the impulsiveness of her heart in urging him to persevere in the ways of the Lord. Catherine wanted to see him perfected in faith and ardent in love; and she wanted Raymond not simply to work untiringly for the Church, but to literally shed his blood for it. Catherine was already preparing some of her best disciples for Raymond when in a few years time he should become the Master-General of the Dominican Order and promote its reform: two women, heroines of holiness, Blessed Maria Mancini and Blessed Chiara Gambacorta, who were attracted to the Dominican life by Catherine's example and on being sent to the famous monastery in Pisa reawakened in the other nuns a real desire for the contemplative life which spread throughout the Order; and many men such as Blessed Giovanni Dominici who became Raymond's right hand in the work of the renewal expecially in Florence and Fiesole. Blessed Raymond who, when Catherine was still living, defended her many times and even favoured her unusual and eyebrow-raising habit of receiving Holy Comunion every day became after her death her most celebrated and loyal biographer to the joy of her other followers. His life of Catherine is lucid, eminently readable and full of Christian wisdom; he tells the straightforward truth and his book, after Catherine's own letters, is the most polished and brightest mirror of her life.

PISA

In 1370, a certain gentleman named Piero Gambacorta became the head of the Pisan government and until his tragic death twenty years later guided it with great wisdom. He had a daughter, a delightful flower of beauty and goodness whose name was Tora, an abbreviation of Theodora and who, at the rather tender age of twelve was married off to a rich youth named Simon Massa. The glowing reports of Catherine's fame had reached the ears of the Gambacorta family and they invited her to their city. She arrived in February 1375 accompanied, as always, by Blessed Raymond, her spiritual daughters and other priests for hearing the confessions of converts. The little group was greeted at the entrance to the city not only by Gambacorta himself and his family, but even by the Archbishop and goodly number of other civil and ecclesiastical dignitaries. Among these illustrious folk was Theodora or Tora, as she was affectionately nicknamed, Gambacorta's favourite daughter, a sweet, gentle girl who was so impressed by Catherine that she immediately joined the group of disciples. During her stay in Pisa, Catherine and her daughters lived as guests in the home of a local nobleman, a certain Gherardo di Buoncorte, whose house was situated near the Church of Saint Christine, in the famous district called Cinica, on the left bank of the Arno river, not far form the Church of Holy Mary of the Thorn. One of Piero Gambacorta's motives for drawing Catherine to Pisa was his hope that her presence and her words would not only bring spiritual benefits to all, but also serve as a salutarly invitation to the many rival political factions to put aside their ferocious hatreds and lay down their arms. And we shall shortly see how in that city Catherine received from her Divine Spouse one of the most sublime manifestations of His love which powerfully encouraged her to persevere in her admirable mission for the Church and civil society. One of her followers, Blessed Giovanni Dominici, in a letter written to her mother who was staying in Venice, has left us a precious description of how whole-heartedly Catherine threw herself into the work of peace-making: "At Pisa I heard her speak to certain sinners; and her sermons were deep, fiery and powerful". And there is no doubt that Catherine's arrival in the important seaport and that the desires she expressed in her private talks with Gambacorta, Buoncorte and other Pisan nobles, inspired them to magnanimously adhere to and help with financial contributions, the "Holy Passage" as she liked to nickname the Crusade against the heathens. Catherine also did her best to make her distinguished hosts understand that success in such a complicated project depended above all on their refusal to join Florence and Milan in the newly created anti-papal League; and, thanks to Catherine's persuasive words, the Pisans – at least, for a while – remained loyal to the Pope, Gregory XI. Power politics however was, quite rightly, very low on Catherine's list of priorities. She had more important things to think about, real flesh and blood people, especially Gambacorta's daughter, Tora who possessed a generosity and an ardour second only to Catherine's own. She listened attentively to and meditated seriously on the irresistible words of the virgin of Siena and, little by little, she began to disattach her heart from the things of this world; and when, only three years later, her husband's death made her a widow, she ignored all new invitations to marriage and consecrated herself totally to God. Tora kept before her mind's eye the incisive phrases Catherine used in order to depict the miserable efforts of those who try to serve the world: "When God cuts away the branch on which they were sitting, they immediately find another one, with the danger of losing God forever… Since God has loosened you from the world, I want you to tie yourself to Him and to marry Christ Crucified with the wedding ring of the holy faith". The voice of Catherine penetrated that large soul with such force, that not only did Tora bravely resist earthly attractions and enthusiastically embrace the Cross of Christ, but also took the Dominican habit and the name Chiara (Clare) becoming like Catherine mother and guide to a slew of holy virgins and promoter in Italy of a fervent return to the ancient discipline in the Dominican Order. After 1380, when Catherine's heavy mantle fell on Tora's physically slender but morally capable shoulders, she made firm friendships with Blessed Raymond of Capua, Blessed Giovanni Dominici and other disciples of Catherine, and worked indefatigably to realize the great Saint's desires. Tora was particularly observant of religious poverty and even refused to accept a tempting, substantial economic contribution from her father for the building of new monastery, preferring to trust only in Providence. Tora died in 1419 and was later officially declared "blessed" by Pius VIII.

THE STIGMATA

In the small Romanesque Church of Saint Christine in Pisa, then as now lapped by the current of the Arno, a certain Crucifix, painted by Giunto Pisano, was venerated by all. Catherine liked to pray before it and often, in the fervour of contemplation, was completely caught up in God, remaining for hours in ecstasy. On April 1, 1375, as she was communing in prayer with her Divine Spouse, Catherine received one of the most sublime communications of Divine Love possible to anyone. Blessed Raymond who was present describes the scene in the following words: "After having celebrated Mass and given her communion, she remained insensible for quite some time. And as I was waiting for her to return to her senses, in order to receive, as often happened, some spiritual consolation from her, in an instant her tiny body, which had been prostrate, little by little, was raised up and, as she was on her knees, she stretched out her arms and hands remaining rigidly for some time in that position with her eyes closed; finally, as if she had been mortally wounded, she suddenly collapsed and shortly after regained consciousness. Then she called for me and said, "You must know, Father, that by the mercy of our Lord Jesus, I already bear in my body his Stigmata... I saw the Crucified Lord coming down towards me enveloped in a blinding light; and by the force of my desire to meet my Creator, my body was made to elevate itself. Then from the scars of His most sacred wounds I saw descending upon me five blood-stained rays, which touched my hands, my feet, and my heart... And I immediately felt such pains in all these parts of my body, especially in my side, that if the Lord had not performed another miracle I don't think that I could have survived such a trial". Accompanied by Blessed Raymond, Catherine just managed to reach Buonconte's house where she was guest and, once again, collapsed as if she was dying. By this time almost all her disciples had heard the news and were gathered anxiously around her weeping for fear of losing her. When she came to herself she repeated to Raymond that if the Lord had not sustained her she would have died instantly. All her followers began praying for their mother and with tears streaming down their faces said: "We well know that you wish to be with your Spouse Jesus; but your reward is already guaranteed; rather, have mercy of us for we are too weak yet to continue by ourselves in the storms of life!". Catherine had to stay in her bed the whole week, and the following Saturday she spoke once again to Blessed Raymond saying: "Father, it seems as if the lord has condescended to grant your prayers: you shall have what you requested". In fact, on Sunday, upon receiving Holy Communion from the hands of Raymond, Catherine went into ecstasy and felt new strength being infused into her. When she retuned to her normal state, she seemed so robust that everybody felt certain their prayers had been answered. Blessed Raymond asked: "Are those wounds imprinted in your body still causing you pain, Mother?". And Catherine: "The Lord has listened to me. Considering the sorrow I feel in my soul, the wounds I have received do not bother but rather comfort me; and where there was affliction, now there is respite: I truly feel it…". Catherine had also obtained another favour from her celestial spouse, that the Stigmata should remain visible.

After having received the supernatural gift of the Holy Stigmata, which certainly helped to increase the interior fire of charity, and zeal and, even, her bodily strength, Catherine committed herself as never before to her superhuman mission for the good of the Church and society. And she went forward in her arduous tasks without losing any of her natural tact and sweetness, but rather growing in humility almost to the total forgetting of herself: it seemed as if she had completely disappeared in order to make room for Jesus Christ whose word of life she was bringing to others with all the fiery, uncontrollable love He had infused into her virginal heart, and she also carried upon her body the miraculous signs of His passion which gave her so much more vigour. Catherine accomplished so much in such a brief span; from the spiritual direction of other common girls like herself who became her first inseparable companions, to the guidance of men, lay and religious, humble and noble, even those who were older and reputed wiser than she, an illiterate girl; from the absorbing work of reforming the religious Orders, to the delicate prodding of powerful princes to their duties; from the same prodding of the clergy, to the reconciliation of warring Tuscan cities among themselves and to the great mission to all Italy and the entire Church; even winning the respectful attention of the Pope himself who showed a certain docility to the voice of this loving daughter as though it were the oracle of God. We may thus say without fear of exaggerating that God himself wanted this great

Saint to dedicate her life to the improvement of the Church and society of the times; and everyone could see that she really made the needs of others her own and that she worked and suffered, offering herself as a victim-soul to God in order to satisfy them. After the episode of the Sacred Stigmata, Catherine's zeal was directed particularly towards the conservation and the increase of fervour in the religious Orders. After her own Dominican Order, which she so richly loved and tirelessly tried to bring back to its antique splendour, Catherine's predilections went to the Carthusians who were already well-known to her, since they had two monasteries only three miles from Siena. Her journey to Pisa gave Catherine the opportunity to know them better and to lavish upon them her affectionate care. On the fertile plain surrounding Pisa, about six miles from the city, there still stands in a place called the Dark Valley, the splendid Carthusian monastery of Calci. This monastery was still under construction during Catherine's time thanks to the offering of a certain Prete Nino Pucci of Spazzavento and a Pisan merchant known simply as Mirante Virginis; and it was further embellished thanks to the contributions of other Pisan noblemen such as Piero Gambacorta. Catherine visited Calci a number of times during her sojourn at Pisa in 1375 and once on her return from Avignon. She enjoyed the edifying conversations of the monks and nourished a sincere love for them and oriented to the Carthusian way of life one of her closest disciples, Stefano Maconi who became the first prior of the Carthusian monastery at Pavia and was, after his death, beatified. Though Catherine's life was as full of apostolic action as anyone else's, she loved to taste the joys of the contemplative life, the complete separation from people and things, acquiring from the fullness of prayer and penance renewed energy for her projects. And even in the midst of these happy moments of devout retirement she continued her apostolatic mission for others with humility and simplicity, igniting in the hearts of her hosts the fire of divine love. Catherine maintained contact with the prior Don Giovanni Lipezzinghi of Calcinaia and some other monks of the establishment by letter and persuaded the Pope, Gregory XI to contribute something to its upkeep. There are still some traces of Catherine's presence in the monastery even today: the Chapel of the Colloquies where she spoke to the monks of heavenly realities, and the precious relic of her finger, jealously guarded by Stefano Maconi and taken by him to the Carthusian monastery at Pontignano near Siena and then to the one at Pavia.

TO THE ISLAND OF GORGONA

In that summer of 1375, Catherine received yet another invitation to visit another place of interest. It came from Don Bartholomew Serafini di Ravenna, prior of the Carthusian monastery recently built on the small island Gorgona, just thirty miles from the Italian mainland. Naturally, Catherine accepted the invitation, and escorted by about twenty followers, including Raymond and some other friars, set sail from Pisa. It was the first time she had ever seen the sea. One call well imagine that mysterious feeling of peace ad tranquillity that descended into her soul when, by slow degrees, almost imperceptibly, the coast vanished from her sight and she found herself surrounded by vast expanse of sea and sky. The rocky island, still far away appeared like a huge solitary fortress lost in that vastitude; but, in fact, it was a refuge, a spiritual oasis for Christian souls aspiring to higher things. They arrived very late and had to spend the first night at a small inn about a mile away from the monastery. The next day, the Prior himself with some of his monks came to welcome Catherine and he immediately beseeched her to make an edifying discourse for them. Catherine, as usual, rose to the occasion and spoke with much sweetness, meekness and goodness. After the impromptu speech-making Catherine went up the rocky, winding path that led to the monastery on high. It was truly the house of God and she was at once enamoured of it during those few days she spent there. She spoke a second time, to the whole community and Don Bartholomew, who was the monk's official confessor, later testified to Blessed Raymond, that each monk received from Catherine exactly that advice or those admonitions that he needed. She came away from Gorgona with a most pleasant remembrance of the place and its inhabitants; and afterwards, whenever she chanced to meet some pious soul desiring to flee from the world and live in holy contemplation and solitude, Catherine always urged him to go to Gorgona. To the Prior of the monastery, the same Don Bartholomew, Catherine left a precious souvenir, her own black mantle or cape which he later brought to the Carthusian monastery in Pavia. In a couple of her letters Catherine refers to him as a "mirror of virtue" and to his community of monks as "good and holy". The monks at Gorgona had their own boat and some of them insisted on escorting Catherine back to Pisa. The return voyage was brief and smooth and as Catherine was disembarking she gave the monks her blessing and said: "If anything should happen during your return trip to Gorgona, do not fear: the Lord is with you". And on the way back, as the little boat was drawing near to the island a furious storm began and after being tossed around here and there by the wind and waves, the little boat was almost smashed to bits on some rocks but, as Catherine had assured them, the storm suddenly ended, a total shipwreck was gratefully avoided and the monks got safely home.

TO LUCCA

Catherine had hardly set foot in Siena after her trip to Pisa when Pope Gregory XI, who had heard so much about her virtues and the power of her words and was so worried about the rebellion of the Florentines who were drumming up support among other Italian city-states, let her know of his desire that she should travel to another Tuscan city, Lucca, in order to persuade its inhabitants to hold fast in their obedience to the Papacy. She had already once written to the magistrates of Lucca, called the Elders, exhorting them to refuse any alliance with Florence and to remain steadfast in their loyalty to the Pope; but in September 1375 she decided to make a personal appearance in Lucca with some of her disciples, including a well-known local minor poet, Ranieri (Neri) di Landoccio. Catherine was received with all due honours and lodged in the house of a certain Bartholomew Balbani.

Her motive, though, was more spiritual than political. Lucca possessed an inestimable treasure: a stupendous Crucifix called "the Holy Visage". The splendid octagonal chapel of the Civitali had not yet been built in the Cathedral of Lucca, but this venerated work of art had been in the city since the eight century, brought there (so it was believed) from Palestine; and even after the Cathedral had been enlarged the famous Crucifix remained in its original place, attracting the devoutful respect and love of all visitors. Catherine also wished to make a pilgrimage to the "Holy Visage"; and on September 14, the Feast of the Holy Cross, she paid homage to the sacred image, as she was swept along by a crowd of the faithful. The Sienese virgin was always moved by the remembrance of the sacred relic and when she wrote to some friends in Lucca afterward she urged them to be full of holy love for God by contemplating that "most sweet and venerable Crucifix". Lucca was famous also for its statue making, especially statues of the Child Jesus. Catherine had formed friendships with other families in Lucca besides the Balbani, in particular with a certain Giovanni Perotti, a dealer in leather goods, and his wife Monna Lippa; and they made a gift to her of one of these statues of the Child Jesus realistically clothed with some lovely colored drapes of their own production. They in turn received a most welcome gift from Catherine; a letter still extant in which she, taking a cue from their statues, speaks about Christ Crucified being our vestment according to the words of St. Paul: "Clothe yourselves with our Lord Jesus Christ"; and she also speaks about the wedding garment mentioned in the Gospels which, covering our nakedness, protects us from the coldness of sin and warms us with that priceless and delectable charity which will bring us to the nuptials of eternal life with God which was manifested to us by the wood of the most Holy Cross.

Catherine also fixed her attention on one of Perotti's daughter who demonstrated an aptitude for the religious life and wrote to him saying: "Bless my little girl for I want her to become a bride of Christ, consecrated only to Him".

MESSENGER OF THE PEACE

Many times during her short life Catherine was chosen by God to calm ferocious hatreds, help others put aside old grudges and to bring the olive branch of peace in the midst of warring factions. She would have preferred to do all this in the solitude of her cell but the Lord preferred that she should do her peace-making in public where everyone could see her. In fact, nobody was more skilled that Catherine in eliminating discord and rooting out hate form human hearts. And hate existed, unfortunately, in frightening abundance in fourteenth-century Tuscany: between entire families who transmitted it to their posterity along with oaths even at the moment of death; and between different cities whose citizens delighted in wicked revenge and in horribly bloody feuds. The same people who blithely forgot or ignored the Christian law of mutual forgiveness, nevertheless had the nerve to enter churches and pray before the altars to God of love and peace.

More often than not, it was the wives, the daughters and the mothers who ran to Catherine in these trying situations; such as Angela Salimbeni, wife of Pietro Belforti, who begged her to reconcile their two grown sons, Benuccio and Bernardo. Sometimes Catherine's disciples acted as go-betweens for the rival factions: such as the celebrated English hermit William Flete who sent her that ferocious fellow Vanni di Ser Vanni who had stubbornly sworn never to sign a peace treaty unless she could do so with the blood of his enemies. But God's love in Catherine conquered all especially when it shone in her eyes as she lifted them up to heaven in prayer and, thanks to the potent words of that Bride of Christ, hearts of ice melted and tears streamed down the family chests covered with thick armour of those who had been erstwhile enemies.

Catherine's sorrow was even more acute and her prayers more heartfelt when she discovered such hatred among the ministers of God. A certain Pietro da Semignano, for example, absolutely loathed one of his confreres in the priesthood. Catherine wrote a letter reminding him that he had been elected to administer the fire of divine charity, the Holy Eucharist; that God had made him a minister of His word which was the word of charity that he had fashioned him into an angel on earth by virtue of the Sacrament of Holy Order; and she pleaded with him "to strip away from your heart and mind all miseries and especially hate… Oh how unpleasant it is to see two priests separated by such mortal hate! It is only a miracle that God does not command the earth to open and swallow you both!".

In her capacity as the angel of peace Catherine had to visit many times various towns that dotted the Sienese countryside such as Montepulciano, Asciano and Montalcino and numerous castles of powerful noble families in constant conflict with one another that dominated the austere hilltops. Her irenic mission brought her into contact with some real experts in power politics when she preached peace to the rulers of Florence, exhorting them to make war on the infedels rather than on their fellow Catholics. It must have been an impressive spectacle to watch this humble young woman of the people go boldly up the celebrated inner staircase of the Palazzo Vecchio in Florence and listen to her heart-piercing harangue demanding that the Florentines cease their rebellion against the Pope and become once again his obedient sons. A couple of years later, as we shall see, Catherine was almost murdered for using such unladylike language. A group of angry Florentines who had been arbitrarily excluded from public office burst into the courtyard of the house where she was staying accusing her of meddling too much in politics and threatening to kill her right then and there. Catherine, with great presence of mind and a calm voice, replied that a bloody martyrdom would be the most welcome and gratifying type of death in the world for herself, so long as her disciples should be spared. The would-be assassins were completely and literally disarmed by Catherine's dignified, imperturbable bearing and quietly went away. She was, however, deeply disappointed about being denied a martyr's death. Nobody who spoke words of peace in those violent times did so quite so loudly and constantly as Catherine because nobody loved God as much as she did. Whenever she saw her efforts crowned with success her heart rejoiced greatly and sung for the victory of the olive branch and in some letters to her followers she even enclosed some pieces of it.

FOR ROME AND CHRIST'S TOMB

Nothing surprises a modern reader of the life of Catherine quite so much as the union and harmony that she managed to achieve between her impetuous heart and her shrewd, native intelligence. Along with her grandiose vision of the situation and the problems of her times she united a sure instinctive grasp of the means necessary to correct them which astonished almost everyone. This was absolutely not due to any book-reading or long experience in practical, hard-headed affairs; Catherine saw things from a higher vantage-point and judged them with a superior certainty thanks to the vigour of her faith and the ardour of her charity which inspired the words pronounced by her lips and, thus, she could say: "God wills it, such has been revealed to me by my heavenly Spouse". Mere human expediency and mundane craftiness were weak and useless in dealing with this strong-willed young woman. This was embarassingly evident – for some people – when Catherine, in her letters and talks with men and women who held the reins of government in their hands, explained her views on sundry matters summing them up in two unalterable propositions which dominated her thoughts. She wanted to se all Christendom united as one family around one centre, the Pope whom she called "the sweet Christ on earth", and she wanted him to return to his natural place of residence, Rome, which she compared sometimes to a homicidal playground, or to a devastated and sterile garden, that she hoped might be transformed into an oasis of peace and a bower full of flowers and fruits.

The main cause of those murderous struggles and of Rome's other problems was the prolonged absence of the Pope. From 1305, Rome had been deprived of its spiritual and political Father. A most unwise decision had moved Clement V to establish his residence in Avignon, a city in southeastern France about sixty-six miles by road from Marseilles. The five Popes who succeeded Clement were, like him, all Frenchmen; but the last of them, Gregory XI, who ruled from 1370-1378 was, in theory, the most unlikely of them all to be energetic and steadfast in his resolution to return to Rome. Elected Pope at only forty years of age, timorous and irritatingly indecisive by nature, he deserved Catherine's stern rebuke: "Act like a man!". Gregory's wishy-washy character was not the only obstacle that impeded him from returning to Rome; the powerful French King did all he could to keep that precious hostage in his own hands and from their strongholds in Italy the various papal representatives were only too glad to cooperate with him. These papal legates were all too often utterly unworthy men who, because of their harsh methods of governing and total lack of loyalty to the Pope, provoked many Italian cities – already much too fanatically jealous of their independence – to open rebellion against the papacy. And when these rebellions exceeded certain reasonable limits, as in the case of Florence, a papal interdict was inevitable; which, in its turn only served to inflame even further the raw sensibilities of the local populations.

Another running sore of Italian political and social life was the existence of angry factions which divided almost every city and town, and ancient rivalries which were never completely extinguished. In many cases, for childish reasons and in private matters, little armies were formed and little local wars were fought; and, by sad necessity there arose the so-called "companies of adventure", headed by fierce men-at-arms whose cunning in directing thousands of other men and cruelty in massacring their enemies and innocent folk, earned them reputations as valiant warriors.

Catherine was painfully aware of all this and her heart was deeply touched by the helplessness and anguished of so many good humble souls, of the disinherited, of the many widows and orphans; and she understood perfectly how much damage was being done to the Church which for too long had had to abandon the idea of promoting a Crusade as the price for allowing itself to get a bit too involved in power struggles which sapped its strength and tarnished its prestige. There was no time to lose and Catherine did her best, according to her lights, to correct the unhappy situation by offering the most efficacious remedies she knew and asking God's help in her prayers to actuate them: the return of the Pope to Rome and a Holy Crusade.

In any case, Catherine wanted a Crusade not only to win back from the sacrilegious hands of the heathens the Holy Sepulchre of Christ, but also to rid Italy of its foulest plague: the legions of mercenaries that stained the flower of her face with the purple testament of bleeding war. The Sienese virgin hoped that these men, mostly foreigners and all hardbitten professionals who, externally at least shared the same Catholic faith, would enthusiastically gather around the banner of the Cross fired by the ideal of trouncing the pagans and, thus, mercifully liberate Italy of their presence. United, they would be invincible against a common enemy and such a holy victory would surely slake their thirsty for military glory. Catherine understood the irresistable appeal of a great and simple idea whose moment has arrived and it immensely pleased her to imagine the Vicar of Christ himself restore to his official seat in Rome issuing the magnificent invitation to all Christian princes and their subjects.

Catherine struggled and literally worked herself to death for these two projects and she had to go to an early grave bitterly disappointed by the knowledge that her efforts had never been fully successful.

THE COUNT

Among the leaders of the mercenary armies during Catherine's time, none was more celebrated and feared than the Englishman John Hawkwood, nicknamed by the Italians as "the Falcon of the Forest". He was the captain of an awesome host of several thousand soldiers, called the Free-Lancers; and he offered, for the right amount of gold, military assistance to any and all of the Tuscan cities who needed it in their terrible internal wars. Wherever they went they left behind wastelands marked by ravaged fields and devastated homes. They earned their living by armed robbery, spreading terror and death everywhere, not sparing even women and children. Cities had to shell out enormous amounts of money in order to save themselves. On June 21, 1375, Florence had to shell out some 130,000 florins in order to get rid of Hawkwood; he then decided to invade Pisa, but the Pisans persuaded him to attack somebody else by paying him 30,500 florins in three installments and so, on July 8 of that same years he made almost unwelcome visit to the Republic of Siena. Fortunately, for Siena that is, St. Catherine sent the powerful warlord a celebrated letter. Pope Gregory XI had already inaugurated a new Crusade by writing two Bulls; one to the superiors of the Dominican and Franciscan Orders and the other privately to Blessed Raymond of Capua. They were ordered to drum up support all over Italy for the Sacred Crusade and to encourage everyone to participate in it. Catherine was delighted.

She immediately perceived, however, that such a grand undertaking would never get off the drawing boards and become a reality unless those mercenary armies that were causing such bloody devastation all over Italy with their internecine wars were stopped and their energies diverted to higher things. With this idea in mind Catherine tried to win over Hawkwood.

She knew that ten years previously, during the reign of Urban V, he had promised to help the Pope in a similar situation by lending his army against the infidels and she wanted to remind him of that promise. Catherine never forgot that often, even in the worst men, there was a pinch of generosity which could become the fountain of good actions and that even they still have a conscience which could bearoused to a salutary remorse. Hawkwood moreover was, externally, a believing Christian, and he just might have gloried in the thought of becoming a true soldier of Christ and atoning for his sins.

While he was encamped near Siena, Blessed Raymond and a companion arrived at his tent and asked permission to speak to him. They were carrying a letter from Catherine who, "in the name of Jesus Crucified and of sweet Mary", had a message for him and his men. The burning desire of the holy virgin was that they should place themselves and their weapons in the service of Christ. "If in order to serve the Devil, you have until now endured hardships and worries", she said, "from this moment on, I want you to change your ways and take up the cause and the Cross of Christ crucified, become the Company of Christ and go fight those heathen dogs, who possess our Holy Land, where the sweet first Truth Himself lived and underwent pain and death for us". She repeated the Pope's appeal and reminded Hawkwood of his own promise made many years ago. "You who are so fond of wars and combat, stop afflicting poor Christians, for it is an offence against God and go fight against those others! It is simply horrible the way we Christians who are members of the body of the Holy Church persecute one another! Thus, you will show yourself stimulus to generosity and the performance of good works". Catherine concluded: "I beseech you, dearest brother, remember how brief your time is in this life".

The fame of this Sienese mantellata who conversed with God and spoke to others in His name, had already reached the ears of John Hawkwood; and he was touched by her letter. The voice of his conscience rebuked him for not having kept his former promise to the Pope and he wondered how Catherine knew about it. He treated the two religious quite affably and in unison with his soldiers swore an oath to join the Crusade as soon as it was definitely organised, saying as much to Catherine in a letter entrusted to Raymond bearing his own seal. The new Crusade was greeted with great enthusiasm everywhere. Catherine was her usual restless self, sending fiery letters to princes and cities and obtaining promises of help for the holy project. And hoping for an early start of what she called the "Holy Passage" she wrote: "I can smell the odour of the flower which is beginning to open!". Unfortunately the pious hopes of so many like Catherine never became reality because of disagreement among the Christian princes and the absence of the Pope from Italy. It is a fact, however, that from that moment on Hawkwood became mush less ferocious and even showed a certain meekness on occasion. He died in Florence in 1394 and was given a sumptuous funeral in the Cathedral of Santa Maria del Fiore and afterwards, a giant frescoe of him on horseback was painted by the artist Paolo Uccello.

Catherine had already died fourteen years previously and undoubtedly her prayers obtained forgiveness for the cruel soldier whom she had once called "her sweet brother in Christ".

The celebrated trial of strength between the Florentine Republic and the Pontiff became, according to the designs of the Divine Providence, the means by which Catherine was able to bring about one of the greatest victories in the history of the Church.

The obstinate rebellion of the Florentins who with their Milanese allies tried to win over to their side the other Tuscan republics, began to weigh heavily upon them. Florence was basically a Guelph city and wished to remain loyal to the Pope, but it had good reasons to complain about the haughty and overbearing papal legates who were suspected of trying to destroy its liberty, and the citizens were beginning to feel the unpleasant effects of the recently imposed Papal interdict. The Florentines slowly realized that their suspicions about the Pope's alleged intentions to invade Tuscany with his armies and become its sole master were totally unfounded, and that their vain attempts to oppose him with violence and to draw other Italian cities to their side were bound to end in failure.

As soon as Catherine heard about what was happening, she tried to calm the agitated spirits and exhorted everyone to work for peace; she especially desired the Pope to be merciful, urging him to conquer the hearts of his rebellious and ungrateful sons with love, and she sent Neri di Landoccio, one of her closest and most trusted disciples, to Avignon with a letter for the Pontiff. In this remarkable letter Catherine expresses her deepest desire in the following words: "Peace for the love of God! If you wish to mete our justice or take revenge, take it our on me, your miserable subject, and inflict on me whatever pain or torment pleases you, even unto death!". She also begged the Pope to send his answer verbally to her by means of the trustworthy Neri. And, as if all this wasn't enough she wrote a letter to two Italian cardinals, Giacomo Orsini and Pietro da Ostia asking them to intercede with the Pope on behalf of the Florentines adding that even if the original troublemakers deserved to be punished, the severe effects of the interdict were doing far more harm to the innocent majority that venerated the Pope as a father.

Unfortunately, many influential people in Florence were becoming more hardened in their obstinacy to Catherine's great sorrow and the Pope's great indignation; and the latter's anger was fanned to a white heat when the Florentine legates, headed by Donato Barbadori, came to Avignon full of arrogance and accusations against him rather than humility and respect.

Gregory XI, therefore, as an extreme remedy, launched his interdict against the rebellious city. When news of the Pope's decision reached Florence, it had a terrible effect on the entire city, not only because of the spiritual, but also because of the material and financial damage it caused, especially to merchants. The common folk were deeply distressed by the folly of their leaders; and the whole populace was convinced that only Catherine, known to be highly influential with the Pontiff and armed with supernatural power and who had already pleaded their cause by letter, could usefully intercede for them. Thus, while still in Siena, she received a written mandate from Niccolò Soderini, head of the Florentine government, to go to Avignon as the official Ambassadress of Florence.

Catherine's employers, however, were skilled dissemblers, especially the so-called Eight or the war-party (Hawks in contemporary parlance), blinded by their passion for political intrigue and persuaded that the unhappy situation had to be settled by arms. Outwardly they were favourable to Catherine's going to Avignon, but in their hearts they were hoping that the Sienese virgin would whitewash their sins before the Pope and make him understand that failure to obtain peace would be entirely his fault. Catherine, in any case, was more than willing to make an effort for the sake of Christian charity, so she accepted her mission for the good of everyone.

It was perfectly clear to her that one of the real causes of all the political and social discords in Italy, including this Florentine one, was the absence of the Pope from Rome; and, since so many evils would simply disappear and so much happiness follow on his return to Rome, Catherine used the occasion to tell him to his face what she had already written to him more than once. "Keep with true and holy solicitude (she had written to the Pontiff) your promise to return… Come and console the poor, the servants of God, your children; we await you with loving desire… Come and do not resist the will of God who is calling you. The hungry sheep are waiting for you to take possession once again of the place held by your predecessor and champion, the Apostle Peter, since, as Vicar of Christ, it is also your one and only proper dwelling… God shall be with you".

Catherine did not forget her other great idea, the Crusade, which all generous souls wished to see led by the Pope who had already approved it. But she was absolutely certain that his invitations to all Christian leaders in this enterprise would be much more efficacious if the Pope were to speak from his natural seat in Rome.

She was anxious, therefore, to depart, full of trust in God. She also sent ahead a letter with Blessed Raymond and some other disciples in April 1376; and at the end of May she finally set out with some other Dominican friars and a few sisters of the Mantellate, twenty-three in all.

On June 18 they arrived at Avignon.

AVIGNON

As soon as the Pontiff learned of Catherine's arrival in Avignon, he provided a comfortable house with a chapel for herself and her sisters and decided that two days later she should attend a concistory and perorate on behalf of the Florentines. She spoke, wielding a charming and captivating Tuscan accent and, as she did so, seemed to go into ecstasy. Blessed Raymond stood at her side and translated her words into Latin. Her words wrought such a powerful effect upon the Pope that at the end of her speech he replied:

"Oh Lady, in order to demonstrate to you how sincerely I desire peace, I leave everything in your hands. I am ready to receive as sons the Florentines, and treat them according to your whishes; but always remember to safeguard the honour and welfare of the Holy Church".

Catherine retuned several times to the Papal palace with Blessed Raymond; and she made a special effort to win over to her side those cardinals and secular rulers who were not interested in concluding a peace. Unfortunately, though, the Florentines were maliciously doing all they could to vitiate Catherine's honest efforts.

The Florentines had promised to send other representives to clarify their intentions to the Pope, but they never arrived and Catherine was so irritated that on June 28 she wrote to the Eight Hawks: "You are ruining everything that is being done here". And in fact, if Florence had really desired peace and if the leaders of the many factions had not heeded the voices of their unruly passions and old rivalries, never again, declared Catherine, could such a glorious peace have been reached, considering the generous mood of the Pontiff. But as soon as he became aware of their delaying tactics and dishonest works, Gregory XI rightly exclaimed: "If the Florentines sincerely wanted peace, they would refrain from doing the smallest act against the will of their Holy Father!". And to Catherine he added: "They are trying to make dupes of you and me".

Finally, the other ambassadors arrived from Florence, Pazzino Strozzi, Alessandro dell'Antella and Michele Castellani. Catherine was, at first, overjoyed by their arrival, but soon realized that they were not about to make an open and total act of submission to Gregory: rather, the conditions for peace they were empowered to offer in the name of their Republic were absolutely unacceptable to the Pope. Before setting out Catherine had told their leaders: "If you want me to handle your affairs, give me permission to offer you as perfectly obedient sons to the Holy Father. This, she continued, is the only way; this is the door through which one must enter". The ambassadors, however, behaved rather differently and when speaking with Catherine or with other papal representatives, never once did they betray what was really in their minds; and Catherine did not err when she made a remark about not finding in them "that affectionate love of peace" which she had found in the Pontiff.

But even if the peace talks with the Florentines were deteriorating quickly, the virgin of Siena was successful in her efforts to obtain her deepest heart's desire: the Pontiff's return to Rome. Before leaving Florence she had sent Blessed Raymond ahead to Avignon with a letter in which she begged Gregory not to delay beyond the end of September and to banish all fears from his mind. And when she arrived at Avignon Catherine used even stronger words in the name of God to convince him to return, even in the presence of the Pope's most powerful opponents who were attempting to undermine his resolve without daring to manifest their opposition in front of Catherine. She was simply marvelous in answering the difficulties raised by the Pope's false advisers and fair-weather friends, and exposing their shameful plots; as when somebody openly hinted at the example of Clement IV who, it was said, never made a move without consulting his cardinals. To which Catherine cited the example of Urban V who, when he saw where his duty laid, never wasted time consulting anyone, but followed his own counsel even if nobody agreed with him.

Thus, Gregory did not allow himself to be unduly impressed by a false letter from a certain Fra Peter of Aragon, a holy servant of God and his great friend (though the Pope had never even heard of this Fra Peter) in which he wrote that Gregory should not go to Italy because his dinner-table might be decked with poison. Poison, Catherine declared, could just as easily be found on the dinner-table at Avignon!... She knew all about the attempted poisoning of Urban V in Avignon, when he had decided to return to Rome! "Go and do not be afraid; God is with you. I have prayed and will continue to pray that the good and sweet Jesus shall banish all base fear from your mind: I order you in the name of Christ to fear not! If you stick your duty, God will be with you and nobody shall prevale against you... Go at once to your Bride who awaits you and restore some colour to her pale visage...". Gregory XI was a timorous man, but an honest one. He had already vowed in his heart to God to go back to Rome, but he dawdled, while Catherine always made up her mind and acted out her decisions very quickly. She learned of the Pope's vow by means of special illumination from on high and wrote to him urging him to stand firm in his holy resolve and to trust in Lord adding: "I hope that you will not despise the prayers that have been offered with such ardent desire and much sweat and tears...".

The Pontiff finally told Catherine openly about his irrevocable will to return to Rome and she replies: "I thank God and Your Holiness that He has strengthened your heart and that he has given you constancy in overcoming all those who wish to block you from returning to your natural home... I pray God that in His infinite goodness He may give me the grace to see you take that first step our the door".

THE CRUSADE

While in Avignon, Catherine's thoughts were not wholly occupied only with the cause of Florence and the return of the Pope to Rome. She took good advantage of her ascendancy over the Pontiff in order to obtain special indulgences and ecclesiastical favours for various Sienese families and her spiritual children, as she revealed in some of her letters to them.

One of the projects closest to her heart was, however, the Crusade against the infedels once the Pope was re-established at Rome. She had already given much time and energy to this project in her letters and particularly, in her talks with the Pisan leader Pietro Gambacorta; and now in Avignon she was able to talk about to Gregory face to face using, as always, Blessed Raymond as her translator.

At one of these audiences, after having listened to Catherine's enthusings, the Pontiff said: "I think it would be better to achieve first peace among Christians and then go on a Crusade". To which, Catherine humbly replied: "Holy Father, you will never find a better way of creating peace among Christians than by means of the Holy Passage. Thus, all these arms that Christians are using against each other shall be used in God's service, to obtain His glory and His forgiveness for our sins. Only the most perverse men will refuse such an opportunity to advance their own salvation. Only in this way can peace be had among Christians who so desire it; and they shall find eternal salvation for their souls".

Charles V was then sitting on the throne of France and Louis, Duke of Anjou, his brother, was more than willing to lead an army in such a Crusade. But the Hundred Years War between France and England was a grave obstacle to such an undertaking. Catherine wrote to the King a letter that combined sweetness and severity, telling him that he must always rule with justice, moderating it though with charity lest he become like a plant without water. He should not consider his kingdom as if it were his private property but as a gift from God to be used for good ends. And speaking about war and the slaughter of countless innocents she exclaimed: "No more, no more for the love of Christ Crucified!". By engaging in his war against England, he had become, said Catherine, "the enemy of a good cause such as the recovery of the Holy Land for which reason, she added, you should be ashamed of yourself, you and all other Christian rulers!... Make peace – she said – and then go make war upon the heathens. Wake up, because the time is short and you do not know when death will come. She had already won over Charles' brother" and therefore, the Saint told the King: "Your brother, the Duke of Anjou, for the love of Christ is willing to work for this holy enterprise. Your own conscience should goad you to follow his sweet example".

On the other hand, Louis was a vain worldly man and Catherine exhorted him to put away all selfish ambitions and control "every disorderly and earthly attachment, for they pass away like the wind and bring death to the soul of he who possesses them", and become a true knight of the Lord. Even though he was younger than Charles, the Sienese virgin also reminded him of the brevity of life and the unreliability of strong youth. After having heard about a sad incident which had occurred a few days previously during a banquet in the Duke's presence, when one of the walls of the room suddenly collapsed killing some of the participants, Catherine redoubled her warnings to him about not wasting his youth in frivolous vices and urged him even more sternly to dedicate his energies to Christ and to see in the incident a divine judgement.

The young Duke was greatful for the Saint's advice and asked her to inform the Pope of his intentions. She wrote to the Pontiff: "If you are still looking for the right man to lead the Crusade, Holy Father, I have found one for you. The Duke of Anjou for the love of Jesus and out of reverence for the Holy Cross wants to commit himself totally to the arduous and holy enterprise; he is waiting upon your pleasure, most sweet Father... His Lordship wishes to discuss these things with you, so please listen to him, for God's love and grant him his heart's desire".

The young Duke's heart was filled not only with the desire to lead a Crusade, but also to see Catherine and in order to talk to her in a more tranquil atmosphere he invited her to his castle at Villeneuve, near Avignon, where the Duchess his wife was staying. The holy virgin stayed at his home for three days and she spoke to the noble couple about the necessity of renouncing worldly vanities and of the joy that the human soul has in serving God. She invited them to cleanse their consciences of their sins and to work unstintingly for the Crusade.

Catherine prayed intensely and unceasingly for the success of the Crusade. Tommaso Petro, one of the Pope's secretaries, wrote down one of the prayers she pronounced during her ecstasy on the vigil of the Feast of the Assumption. A certain Fra Tommaso Buonconti of Pisa who also watched her on the occasion tells us that "she was so alienated from her senses and so rigid that it would have been easier to break her body than to bend it...". While speaking to the Lord in prayer she said, among other things: "I have a body which I return and offer up to you; here is my flesh and my blood; rip me apart and destroy me for the sake of those for whom I pray. If it is your will, smash every bone in my body for the sake of your Vicar on earth, the bridegroom of your bride... create a new heart for him, make him grow always in grace, make him strong so that he may hold aloft the banner of the most Holy Cross, so that even the heathens may participate with us in the fruits of the passion and blood of your only- begotten Son, the immaculate Lamb".

THE POPE'S RETURN TO ROME

In that unhappy year of 1376, the obstacles that were blocking the Pontiff's road back to Rome seemed so many and so difficult to overcome, especially the rebellion of Florence and the other Italian Republics against the Papacy.

Many ecclesiastics wanted the Pope to wait for these storms to calm down before going back to Rome, but Catherine, on the contrary, firmly believed and hoped that they would be immediately calmed by means of such a return of the Papacy to its natural residence. With the hindsight of history we may say that the facts were on her side and certainly, divine providence was at the helm guiding a floundering humanity; and Catherine was elected by God as his instrument or as an angel sent by Him to help His vicar on earth to complete the work that had to be done.

Even before leaving for Avignon, the Saint had written to the Pontiff with assurance: "Come; I tell you that those ferocious wolves will lower their heads on your lap like gentle lambs; and they shall ask for your mercy, Holy Father". And she told him the same thing once he finally decided to return to Italy.

Catherine's prayers undoubtedly helped to hasten that happy day. Cheerful and confident as always, she set out with her followers overland towards Tolone. As soon as she arrived there she was surrounded by an enthusiastic crowd and even the local bishop paid her a visit. A young mother of great faith who was carrying her sick child in her arms approached Catherine and aroused such pity in her that she instantly healed it. The Saint and her group then continued their long journey by sea in order to avoid similar delays, but a storm forced them to drop anchor at Saint-Tropez. They once again began travelling by land and on October 3 stopped in Varazze in order to visit the home town of Catherine's famous confrere Blessed Giacomo who had been Archbishop of Genova and author of the celebrated book *Leggenda Aurea*; she found the city, however, devastated by the plague and she advised the citizens to build a chapel in honour of the Holy Trinity, adding a promise that their city would never again be visited by such a loathsome disease. And her promise became reality.

The Pope had begun his journey by sea on the advice of Catherine; he had already constructed a ship on the Rodan without telling anyone why and, suddenly, on September 13 he left the palace. Very few people realized what was happening at first; but all opposition was finally useless, even that of Gregory's aged father who threw himself down on the palace steps in the hope of blocking his son. Catherine's potent words were still sounding in his ears, drowning out those of his own flesh and blood just as Gregory also ignored the pleadings of all the citizens of Avignon among whom the news of this departure had quickly spread like a flash of lightening. The Pope stopped at Marseille where the cardinals caught up with him, and after a stay of twelve days, a fleet of twenty-two ships with all of them aboard, set sail for Italy on October 2. A furious storm which seemed sent by the Devil himself struck them as they approached Monaco, but as

God willed, on October 18 the fleet dropped anchor at Genova.

Then some new problems arose. News arrived from Rome about violent riots that were supposed to have taken place thanks to rumours noised abroad by some malcontents in Florence concerning the Pope's intentions. At this point Gregory hesitated, while his cardinal suggested, naturally, that he should go back to Avignon. But on hearing that Catherine was also in Genova he visited her secretly, by night, in order to avoid unnecessary observation and comments by the local populace. He had nobody and nowhere else to turn to for help; Catherine was the only person who could advise him on what to do in his unenviable situation. She was, as usual, locked in her room, praying fervently and offering herself as a holocaust for the good of the Church. When Gregory walked in, she threw herself at his feet in total confusion. We cannot even imagine what expressions she used, literally from the bottom of her heart, begging God to give special courage to his Vicar on earth. The Pontiff felt consoled and refreshed after his meeting with Catherine and, without consulting anybody, recommenced his journey on October 29 eventually reaching Leghorn where he was welcomed by the Lord of Pisa, Piero Gambacorta. The Pope remained with his host for eight days and then set sail once again towards Piombino. He disembarked on November 25 and continued his journey by land and by December 5 was at Tarquinia in the Papal States.

Here a letter reached him from Catherine who was still in Genoa exhorting him to persevere against everyone and everything and assuring him of God's constant protection, "I tell you that the sooner you arrive at your destination, the seat of the glorious apostles Peter and Paul, the sooner God will help you to do so. Put your trust in the prayers of the true servants of God who are interceding so much for you".

While plans were being made at Tarquinia for Gregory XI's solemn entrance into Rome, Catherine decided to stay in Genoa to comfort two of her closest disciples who had fallen gravely ill: Neri di Landoccio and especially Stefano Maconi who had been reduced to an extreme state. He was being literally devoured by an acute fever when Catherine visited him in his room with his confessor and some of her Mantellate. The Saint asked him how he was doing and he jokingly replied: "Some people say that I am being sorely tried, but I don't know by what". Catherine touched his forehead and said "Listen to my little son! He has a fever that is consuming him and doesn't even know it! Come, Come, I want you to be healed: get up and begin working again with the others". And Stefano got up and cheerfully resumed his normal life.

When all was ready Catherine left Genoa for Leghorn and, after a brief stop there, went to Pisa where she disembarked to visit her elderly mother, impatient as ever to see her daughter. She remained at Pisa for a month and had great pleasure in seeing some old friends once again; the good Fathers of Saint Catherine, the Carthusians at Calci and many other disciples, especially the young widow, Tora Gambacorta, one of her most serious pupils in the ways of Christian perfection. From Pisa she finally arrived in Siena towards the end of December or, perhaps, the beginning of January of the following year.

Meanwhile all the preparations had been completed at Tarquinia and at Rome. Although it had degenerated into desolation and poverty because of the Pontiff's long absence, Rome managed to cloth itself in its former splendour. After leaving Ostia on January 17, 1377, the Pope sailed up the Tiber, lined by cheering crowds and reached the Basilica of Saint Paul where he disembarked for the last time and processionally made his grand entrance into the heart of the ancient city. The clergy and the whole populace turned out to greet him, many weeping for joy; the streets were strewn with flowers and everyone took up the shout "VIVA GREGORIO!" which was nearly drowned out by the ringing of all the bells: at the Porta San Paolo, the Senate reverently offered him the keys to the city.

Thus, after seventy years, the Apostolic See was once again established in Rome ending what many writer have called "the Babylonian Captivity".

The Pastor had returned to his flock and Catherine, in her bare little room in Siena, gave thanks to the Lord.

NICCOLÒ DI TULDO

Ensconced once again in her native city, Catherine would have liked to have passed the rest of her life in silence and retirement; but, once again she was called hither and thither to bring words of peace and to pour into hearts the balm of consolation. Her voice, her affectionate looks, the sighs that issued forth from her breast, and the loving conversations she had with God and which she shared with her listeners, simply overwhelmed even the most obstinate souls.

The greatest demonstration of her compassion towards sinners, though, was in the episode of Niccolò di Tuldo. He was a fiery youth from Perugia, who was accused of having plotted with some friends against the rulers of Siena and was subsequently arrested and condemned to death.

It was in April, 1377, and a certain Father Caffarini went to see the unhappy young man, hoping to hear his confession and, instead, he found Niccolò running back and forth in his cell like a madman. His desperate situation made him hurl the most horrendous blasphemies against God and the worst cursing against the priests who tried to induce him to repent of his sins before he died. Finally, Catherine was summoned to come and do what she could and in a letter to Blessed Raymond, she described how the youth met his end: "I went to visit him, of whom you have already heard, and he felt such comfort and consolation that he made his confession and disposed himself very well, making me promise, for the love of God, that at the moment of justice, I should be with him, and so I did. The next morning, before the ringing of the bell, I went to see him and for the first time in many years he received Holy Communion. His will was in total harmony and obedience to God's will, but he was still afraid to face death... But the unlimited and efficacious goodness of God strengthened him, creating in him such a burning love and desire for God that he could not live without Him saying: 'Stay with me, don't leave me and I shall be well and die happy' and then he laid his head upon my bosom. I also felt happy and even breathed the odour of his blood and of my own which I desire to shed for my sweet spouse Jesus.

I felt this desire growing in my soul and I also sensed his fear, as I said: 'Don't worry, my sweet brother, because very soon we shall arrive at the nuptials: you shall go bathed in the blood of the sweet Son of God... I shall be waiting for you at the moment of execution'.

Just think, Father, how all fear was banished and sadness transformed into joy; he was almost ecstatic, exclaiming: 'Where is all this grace coming from that I should feel such peace of soul, though death be imminent?'. He was so enlightened that he called the executioner's block holy and said: 'I shall go to it strong and happy even if the event were a thousand years hence, just knowing that you will wait for me there' and he said other things so sweet to hear about the goodness of God, that would make one weep.

I waited for him, therefore, at the place and seeing me he began to laugh and wanted me to make the Sign of the Cross over him and when I had done so I said: 'Now to the wedding feast, my dear brother, for very soon you shall reach eternal life'. He knelt down with great sweetness and as I fitted his head on the block, I placed my mouth next to his ear and reminded him of the blood of the Lamb. He kept repeating 'Jesus' and 'Catherine' and as he was speaking, I received his head into my arms, thinking all the while of God's mercy…".

Catherine also added that she was the young man's soul fly heavenward and that she envied his death. Her white habit had been sprinkeld by his blood, and she said: "I hated to have had to wash away the stains".

ROCCA D'ORCIA

Catherine was always anxious to seek and delighted to find souls that had seemed lost forever and bring them back to the Lord; and after her brief stay in Siena, she accepted an invitation to visit the awesome castle at Rocca d'Orcia which was situated on an outcropping of the mountain Amiata The castle was the seat of the great Salimbeni Family, fierce rivals of the equally powerful Tolomei Family.

Two daughters of the Salimbeni faction had recently lost their husbands during a violent skirmish and they were seriously thinking of entering the cloister. Their mother, Monna Bianchina, though deeply sympathetic towards their plight, wanted to keep them at home with herself and begged Catherine to help her to accomplish this. As usual, the Saint never ignored an opportunity to exercise her considerable peacemaking prowess.

She left for the "Rocca" in the autumn of 1377 with several disciples including Blessed Raymond, Tommaso della Fonte and Bartolomeo Dominici and as usual, succeeded marvelously in re-establishing peace among the rival families. Hatred disappeared, disagreements were forgotten and promises of moral amendment were really kept. The sight alone of Catherine was enough to soften the hardest of hearts and to reawaken the desire for friendship between former enemies.

One of the worst features of life in the Sienese countryside was the existence of small private armies in the service of great families like the Salimbeni. They were really only bands of outlaws who cared nothing for religion or morality and lived by robbery, a way of life shared even by their women and children.

The coming of Catherine was like the sudden appearance of an angel. Even those people had spiritual souls that had to be saved. A great crowd swarmed around the hillside fortress to hear Catherine speaking: most came because of a vague curiosity which soon became a sincere desire to listen. Never before had they heard anybody speak such moving words! Catherine's mere presence, her exhortations, her ardent prayers and humble advice entered those hardened hearts and reawakened their sense of Christian piety. The throng kept growing at an amazing rate and so thick was the press that five priests had to come to help the first three hear all the confessions.

During this period Catherine also revealed a singular talent for dealing with possessed people. The enemy of the human race thought he had found plenty of adherents, in that region, but Catherine freed them all with a simple Sign of the Cross. One poor possessed fellow, who was so absolutely uncontrollable that not even a dozen men could hold him down, was brought up to the "Rocca" with his hands and feet in chains. They led him into the courtyard and sent for Catherine. As soon as she arrived and saw him she asked: "What has this poor man done that he should be so cruelly chained? I beg you, in the name of Jesus Christ, unchain him and do not be afraid". And then, with her eyes lifted heavenward she came beside the man as he lay on the ground like one dead. Catherine said to the onlookers: "Give him some food, don't you see that he is hungry?". The unhappy fellow managed to sit upright and looked around at the bystanders. His eyes met Catherine's eyes and she made the Sing of the Cross over him. Like a sweet little lamb, he ate something and joyously returned to his family.

The Saint prolonged her stay at Rocca d'Orcia for another four months and in Siena the gossips prolonged their uncharitable comments about her. Some even speculated that Chaterine was staying there in order to build up her own faction and lead a conspiracy of nobles against the Sienese republic. She immediately wrote a letter to the Magistrates and to some of her disciples, in which she denounced suck wicked slanders attributing them to the Devil himself who was trying to obtain revenge against Catherine for the loss of so many of his followers; and she added: "I came up here to save souls and I would sacrifice my life a thousand times to do so if it were necessary for their sake. The spirit of God is calling me and I follow His inspiration. And if they continue their calumnies and persecutions I shall continue my tears and prayers...".

After leaving Rocca d'Orcia, Catherine went to Sant'Antimo, Montepulciano, Castiglioncello and to the Castle of Belcaro which Nanni di Ser Vanni had given to her so that she could transform it into a monastery for cloistered nuns. And everywhere she went, people came to see her and were moved to compunction for their sins. The priests who accompanied her heard confessions all day and even late into the night, absolving penitents of all their sins. It was a tiring work, but they were comforted by the words of Catherine and by the wonders of God's grace.

FLORENCE

There was, however, no rest for Catherine; she soon had to return to the field of battle for the good of the Church. Gregory XI had returned to Rome without difficulty; but the hostile attitude of the Florentine leaders who still refused to bow their heads and ask for peace, was like a thorn in his heart. For more than a year now the unhappy city had lain prostrate under the papal interdict: the churches were closed, the faithful could not receive the sacraments and all religious ceremonies had ceased completely. The Pope had hoped that such a draconian measure would help him obtain the city's obedience; Catherine also shared this hope and had written to the Eight announcing the Pontiff's return to Italy: "The Pope is going back to Rome, he is coming bach to this Bride, to the place of Saints Peter and Paul! Run to greet him with a humble heart!". She understood that peace was absolutely necessary. All the good fruits of the Pope's return to Rome would be lost unless some sort of political tranquillity was restored to the Italian city-states, especially Florence. Catherine wrote to Gregory suggesting that he would grant an audience to some of the Florentine leaders who wanted to talk to him. He was well aware, though, that most of the other leaders were intensely ill-disposed towards him and unwilling to submit to his conditions. The Florentines saw the Pope as the destroyer of their freedom and in this they were partly right when they witnessed the unheard-of cruelties practiced by the Bretons who had previously been sent by the Pope into Italy. Catherine hoped and worked with all her strength for peace and was deeply displeased to see so much money spent on soldiers rather than on the poor; but the Pope, allowing himself to be swayed by the French cardinals, insisted on bending the Florentines to his will by the threat of arms. Thus, for a while, both sides waged a war of nerves.

The Florentines, however, made an unbelievable mistake when, at the instigation of their leaders, they publicly violated the Papal interdict. When Angelo da Ricasoli, the bishop of Florence, who had left the city upon orders from Gregory XI, was invited to return under pain of amends, he refused, paid the fines and won praise from Catherine for his constancy. The so-called Eight of War had become so powerful that on October 22, 1377 they commanded a solemn Mass to be celebrated in the Piazza della Signoria by some reluctant but cowed priests. This flagrant and scandalous violation of ecclesiastical prescriptions certainly merited an exemplary punishment from the Pope; Catherine, however, still pleaded with Gregory to use mercy promising him that Florence would submit to him in the end. She never desisted interceding for the Florentines and begged the Pope to lift entirely the interdict which had been so contemptuously disobeyed.

The Saint realized, on the one hand, that the fault laid with a small group of ill-disposed persons, not with the majority of good people that groaned and suffered in respectful and religious silence under the interdict; on the other hand, she saw how necessary peace was for all Italy and how the lack of it was a great hinderance to the Pope in his efforts to reform the Church and begin a Crusade. Catherine wrote to the Florentines: "Run, run to the arms of your Father. If you do so, you shall have peace, spiritually and socially, you and all Tuscany… I want you to be docile sons, not rebels, obedient subjects for the rest of your lives! My brothers, I tell you with pain and tears from my heart that you are dead! Do not think that God shall overlook the insults offered to his Bride…". She also told Gregory very frankly not to declare war, but to accept peace at any price, even if the Florentine leaders were obstinate in their disobedience.

"You must beat them with the stick of benignity, love and peace rather than with that of war. Do not look at their ignorance, the blindness and the arrogance of your sons. With peace you shall extinguish from all hearts war, rancor and division". She was always thinking of the many souls that could be lost and of the danger of inflamed hatreds, and she put all her trust in the strength of love and forgiveness which conquers all human obstacles and has greater authority than the most sophisticated weapon.

THE COSTA DI S. GIORGIO

Everybody knew that the hostilities of Florence against the Papacy were the creation of a small group of factious men that had seized the reins of power; even Blessed Raymond of Capua was well-aware of what was going on when, in 1377, he paid a visit to the influential Florentine, Niccolò Soderini, a sincere admirer of Catherine, who by now placed all his trust in her wisdom and charity, considering the immense prestige she enjoyed with the populace. Catherine tried her best to convert the rebels and had summoned her closest disciple Stefano Maconi, from Siena in order to help her. He was only twenty-seven years old, but he was an accomplished speaker and he knew just what words to use in rebuking the Florentine leaders for having sent Catherine to Avignon as their ambassadress of peace, while secretly plotting against her behind her back. Some of the leaders were willing to listen to reason, but all the others remained hardened in their opposition and, Stefano, had to flee from the city when the rabble was incited by them against him.

Blessed Raymond, meanwhile had been elected prior of the Dominican House, Santa Maria sopra Minerva in Roma and he was thus able to speak face to face with Pope Gregory about these problems. In these audiences he strongly reaffirmed his great trust in Catherine and expressed his conviction that if she were allowed to go to Florence once again the problems would be quickly resolved and he also asked the Pope permission for himself and a few other friars to accompany her. The Pope, however, trusted only Catherine and denied Raymond's request. Catherine offered no resistance to the Pontiff's command; for her, his voice was the voice of God. She left Siena for Florence after having sent a letter announcing her arrival to the Minister of Justice and other officials.

Christmas was at hand, and thinking about how the Florentines, because of the interdict were still being deprived of the sacraments, she tried to arouse their desire for that heavenly food which only the Vicar of Christ could give. "Do not harden your hearts, but humble yourselves now while you still have time; for the soul that humbles itself shall always be exalted. We are not Jews or Saracens, but Christians baptised and ransomed in the blood of Christ. Arise then and run into the arms of the Father. This is the Pasch I desire to share with you". Accompanied by Stefano Maconi, Catherine arrived in Florence on December 13, 1347. She understood at once, though, that hatred had unfortunately hardened those Florentine hearts so much that there was nothing left to hope for. Everyone was too caught up in the labyrinth of political intrigues and the heat of political passions to listen to Catherine, and even the leaders of the Guelf party, who were basically favorable to some kind of reunion with the Pope, practically ruined such a possibility by maintaining their bitter hostility towards the other parties. The, on March 27, 1378 news reached Florence of the death of Gregory XI. Peace talks were immediately suspended until the first week of May; and Catherine was overjoyed to see the election of a new Pope, Bartholomew di Prignano, who named himself

Urban VI. He was elected on April 8 and solemnly enthroned in Saint Peter's Basilica on the 18 of the same month, which was also Easter Sunday. Catherine had another reason to be happy when Silvestro de Medici, the new Minister of Justice, sent some ambassadors at the beginning of May to resume the peace talks.

In Florence itself, unfortunately, the hatreds grew and the struggles intensified. The whole populace was involved and in the midst of that unhappy confusion the most furious were the members of the Ghibelline party who continually roamed about the streets looking for and threatening to rough up members of the other parties, especially the Guelfs. Among their targets were Niccolò Soderini and Ristoro Canigiani who were close and affectionate friends of Catherine; their houses were set on fire and, as if that were not enough, Catherine herself was accused of being the main cause of all the disorders. At that time Catherine was living in a small house, built for her special use by Soderini, near the foot of a slope called San Giorgio beyond the Arno and, one day as she was spending some time indoors with her disciples, a ferocious gang of miscreants broke into the house shouting: "Let's grab that wicked woman and burn her intruders alive!". The frightened housekeepers allowed the intruders to enter while Catherine and her little group hid in the garden at the back of the house. The would-be murders, uttering threats of death, ran through all the rooms looking for her, when finally and quite calmly Catherine appeared in front of them, fell down on her knees, raised her head heavenwards and exclaimed: "Here I am, take me and kill me. But I beg you, in the name of God, do not touch my little ones". These words, Catherine later told Blessed Raymond, were like a knife that cut right through to the heart of the would-be assassin who lost the courage even to touch her as if his hands had been tied, and he simply replayed: "Get away from here at once". But Catherine, who desired nothing more than martyrdom said: "No, I will stay right here for I have always looked forward to this moment, to give my life for God".

The hired killers abruptly left the house without harming anybody, and Catherine sadly reflected: "Oh miserable me! I am not worthy to be a martyr! I do not deserve to have my blood poured out for the Mystical Body of the Church!".

THE OLIVE BRANCH TO FLORENCE

As the political fighting continued along its furious way in Florence, Catherine was advised by her disciples to leave the ungrateful city; she listened to them but did not want to abandon her sincere efforts to establish peace. She agreed to spend a few days in a mountain retreat in the Florentine hinterland, near the monastery of Vallombrosa; and writing to her dearest disciples, Alessia Saracini, her sister in the Dominican Third Order, she told her to pray and to have prayers she said: "Have prayers said at various monasteries. Tell our Prioress to have our daughters recite special prayers for peace, so that God may show His mercy towards us".

Catherine then wrote to the new Pontiff, whom she had already met in Avignon and, continuing her efforts to obtain peace, said in her letter: "I beg you and command you, for the love of Christ Crucified, to mercifully welcome back the sheep that have strayed from the flock (because of my own sins); this is the only way to soften their hardness of heart, with a show a gentleness and holiness". And foreseeing the Pope's main difficulty, their incredible stubborness, added: "If they do not ask for peace, may your Holiness grant it anyway. Doubt not that afterwards they will become your best children".

Urban received this letter while he was at Tivoli with four of his Italian cardinals. He realized that there was not a moment to lose; in fact, he had had a vague presentment, which rapidly became a terrible certainty, that the French cardinals, were planning to desert him. Of the sixteen cardinals who had participated in the recent conclave, four were Italian, only one was Spanish and all the others were French. Catherine understood the danger and quickly tried to eliminate it. To Cardinal De Luna, who shortly afterwards betrayed Urban, she wrote a letter informing him that she had advise the Pope not to waste time: "Do not delay in applying a remedy, for the boulder is about to fall on somebody's head".

She had heard about the disagreements that had arisen among he French cardinals during the summer of that year: "All of which – she said – is an intolerable sorrow for me, because of my fear of heresy [she was really referring to the threatened schism], which undoubtedly will take place thanks to my sins". She also wrote to the Pontiff, once again urging him to act quickly to reform the garden of the Holy Church, "with good and virtuous plants" and to create "a company of good cardinals who will work not to increase their personal greatness but as true pastors", who will lead their sheep, who will be "pillars" of strength, who will help the Pope in his "weighty affairs".

The schism, however, was by now inevitable and, if it occurred while Florence and its allies were still in enmity with the papacy, it would cause unimaginable harm to all Italy. This was the main reason for which Catherine worked so tirelessly for peace at any price between the Pope and Florence. The supreme interests of the Church and of Italy were at stake and Catherine had the merit of having understood it all. And she also understood the lack of sincerety and false zeal of the French cardinals who whispered words of revenge in the Pope's ear against Florence and her Tuscan allies under the pretext of defending the honour of the Catholic Church.

Catherine's pleadings finally prevailed upon the Pontiff. On July 18 his messenger entered Florence bearing the traditional olive branch and the entire city rejoiced. Catherine, who was present, thanked the Lord in her heart and wishing the same joy for her fellow citizens of Siena, wrote to Sano di Maco and her other disciple: "The dead sons have been resurrected, the blind see, the dumb speak, crying out in a loud voice: Peace, peace, peace! Now he is called the sweet Holy Lamb, Christ on earth, who before was called heretic and Patarin… The olive branch arrived Saturday evening… and I am sending one to you also". Thus she concluded the letter with some actual leaves of olive for the comfort of her followers.

On July 28 the real peace talks began; the Florentines accepted the Pope's conditions and the interdict was lifted. Catherine left for Siena; all the insults, the hardships and treacheries she had had to endure were forgotten; she was simply glad that peace had returned.

Siena - Basilica of San Domenico - Chapel of the Vaults.
Portrait of St. Catherine (detail)   (A. Vanni 1332-1414)

Siena - *Basilica of San Domenico* - View from the south.

Siena - Basilica of San Domenico
Catherine heals a possesed woman   (A. Vanni, XVI century)

Siena - Basilica of San Domenico
Chapel of St. Catherine - frescoes by Antonio Bazzi called Sodoma (1526) and by Francesco Vanni (1596)

Siena - Basilica of San Domenico
The Relic of St. Catherine's Head
with marble dossal
(G. di Stefano XV century)

Siena - Basilica of San Domenico
Chapel of St. Catherine - *The Saint in Ecstacy* (detail)

(Sodoma - Giov. Antonio Bazzi)

Siena - House of St. Catherine: *Arcades and Basilica of San Domenico in the distance*

Siena - Shrine - House of St. Catherine:
Altar of the Most Holy Crucifix

Siena - Shrine - House of St. Catherine:
Crucifix of the Stigmata (1300)

Siena - Room of St. Catherine's House at the Shrine - House.
The Saint absorbed in prayer, going up the stairs without touching the steps.

(A. Franchi, 1898)

Siena - Room of St. Catherine's Shrine at the Shrine - House.
Catherine praying on her knees as a radiant dove descends upon her head.

(A. Franchi, 1898)

Siena - Room of St. Catherine's House at the Shrine - House.
Catherine cuts off her hair in the presence of Father Tommaso della Fonte.

(A. Franchi, 1898)

Siena - Room of St. Catherine's House at the Shrine - House.
Catherine holding the Infant Jesus in her arms as Our Lady watches.

(A. Franchi, 1898)

Siena - Room of St. Catherine's House at the Shrine - House.
Catherine recognises Jesus in the guise of a beggar to whom
she gives some of her fatehr's clothes. (A. Franchi, 1898)

Siena - Room of St. Catherine's House at the Shrine - House.
The Mystical Marriage of Jesus with Catherine on the Last Day of Carnival, 1367.

(A. Franchi, 1898)

Roma - Basilica of St. Mary over Minerva: **St. Catherine's sarcophagus.**

THE DIALOGUE

With a heart full of consolation, Catherine returned to her little cell in Siena for a few months of tranquillity, during which her ecstasies became more frequent and more prolonged. She would remain quite insensible during these mystical experiences while the tongue was the only part of the body she could freely move; and it must have been a truly remarkable occasion for any onlookers to see and hear her as she conversed with her Divine spouse, sometimes cheerfully, sometimes weeping.

"O love, o love", she would cry out, "you are the sweetest thing there is, you allow us to have a foretaste of the good and joyous things that we hope to enjoy more fully without ever being satiated in eternal life. O everlasting beauty, hidden so long from the world! O eternal love, grant me the consolation to see all hearts forced open by the strength of your love! I want to enlighten my beloved children: Lord, tear down the wall that divides you from them, so that they may love you totally!".

Catherine's words were addressed now to the Eternal Father, now to the Word Incarnate and she even seemed to change colour: sometimes her face became as white as snow, other times as red as fire; and whoever saw her in these moments felt tears of devotion come to their eyes. Catherine was usually helped by four secretaries: Neri di Landoccio, Barduccio Canigiani, Stefano Maconi and Cristoforo di Gano, all of whom gathered from her own lips such treasures of priceless teachings which, put together, formed an entire book commonly called *The Dialogue*.

It was completed on October 13, 1378, only three months after it was begun. It is usually thought that Catherine, while in ecstasy with her eyes fixed heavenwards, dictated the greater part of it in a small chapel of the hermitage near Siena where she often went. Another famous local worthy and great servant of God, a certain Brother Santi, lived there; and Father Tommaso Caffarini declared solemnly that more than once he saw the holy Sienese virgin utterly absorbed in God while her disciples wrote down her words.

This exquisite book is the ripe fruit of a soul who continually lived in the presence of God and, with good reason, called *The Dialogue*, because it is essentially the faithful record of a prolonged conversation in an ecstasy of love between Catherine and God, which explores the depths of Christian spirituality. The work has had, however, various titles such as *Treatise of Divine Revelation* and it has the following basic structure: a prologue consisting of eight chapters and four longer sections or treatises; on Discretion, on Prayer, on Providence and on Obedience. The longest is the one, on Prayer, which contains the splendid sub-section "Treatise of Tears".

This book, no less than Catherine's letters is "a monument of wisdom". And it is remarkable how, without any formal schooling, an illiterate young woman, unlike so many grave divines of her time, was able to scale the heights of mysticism and move and breathe in such a rarefied spiritual atmosphere for so many years while immersed at the same time in so many worldly affairs. Pope Pius II was right when he said that Catherine's doctrine was not acquired but infused directly by God, because only He could have given the Sienese virgin such a high and perfect knowledge of His divine perfection, of the sublime excellence of the virtues and of the most efficacious way of arriving at a perfect love of God in this life.

This marvellous book, with her letters, has won for Catherine a secure place among the Doctors of mysticism and among the most eminent Masters of Christian perfection. Her words are not of men, but of God; no other teaching could ever be found in her, save that which springs directly from the fountainhead of divine revelation, for Catherine could neither see nor relate anything which she had not seen with her own limpid gaze in that immense sea of light to which God had raised her.

Thus was she made worthy to become the incomparable guide and outstanding mother of souls with her writings, by means of which she still prolongs the mission that God entrusted to her for the advantage of the whole Church.

THE EUCHARIST

All the spiritual vigour that characterized St. Catherine came to her from that perennial centre of light and life, the most Holy Eucharist. This heavenly bread was, literally, her life, for all her early biographers fully agree that it sustained her spiritually and materially; and it must be truly said that her entire earthly life was one great eucharistic miracle. "By the power of the Holy Eucharist – wrote Cornelius a Lapide – she became an angelical virgin in such wise as to be called the wonder of the ages". For many years, from the first day of Lent to the feast of Ascension, the Divine Sacrament was her only food: it was quite sufficient to satisfy her, and when because of illness or other serious reasons she could not receive it, she felt such an intense hunger for it, that she begged her confessor with tears in her eyes: "Father, I am hungry; for the love of God, give food to my soul".

In order to satisfy the desire she had to receive the celestial bread every day, Pope Gregory XI granted her the priviledge of using a small portable altar which is still preserved today among her other relics in the Church of San Domenico in Siena. The priests who accompanied Catherine on her journeys celebrated Mass early in the morning wherever she happened to be lodging and, after having received Holy Communion, she would remain immobile for many hours and her heart would beat so strongly that everyone heard it.

Wondrous things occurred during these Holy Communions. While it was still in the hands of the priest, the Sacred Host would move by itself and, sometimes, abruptly fly from them and place itself on Catherine's tongue. She often saw, as she solemnly declared, Jesus himself in the form of a small boy in the Host; the altar appeared to her gaze as though it were surrounded by angels and at times it seemed to be enveloped by flames as the burning bush did to Moses. At these moments the visage of the Sienese virgin was transfigured: whoever saw her thought she was a seraphim. Indeed angels themselves sometimes brought Catherine Holy Communion even when no priest was present, bearing the sacred species on a white cloth; and she used to reveal to others that sometimes, for several days, the taste of blood stayed in her mouth.

An interesting episode took place in Lucca in 1375. A certain priest who didn't believe all the extraordinary things that people told him about Catherine decided to put her to the test by means of a gross imposture. She was in bed, unwell; and the said priest came to visit and asked if she wished to receive Holy Communion. Catherine accepted the offer most willingly; so the priest returned to his Church, took a small pyx, placed an unconsecrated host in it, and then with a great show of candles, songs and a procession of people carried it back to the house where Catherine was staying. As he entered the room, he noticed that while everyone else fell to their knees, she did not make any outward sign of reverence, but seemed rather disturbed and even angry.

The priest was on the point of scolding her as a woman of little faith; but she, inflamed with holy zeal, rebuked him for having tried to sacrilegiously trick her with common bread. The unworthy priest left, humiliated and derided by all; and Catherine was consoled by a vision of angels who miraculously gave her a real Holy Communion.

In the dialogue and the letters, the holy virgin says many beautiful things about the Most Holy Sacrament; in fact one could put together an entire treatise on the Eucharist from the various passages in which she speaks about it. St. Paul and St. Thomas Aquinas are her obvious masters in these matters and she even conversed with these two saints about it in her visions.

The devotion to Jesus in the Blessed Sacrament was one that transported Catherine to Jesus Crucified of whom she was a living image. That which she said about another person in particular was indeed applicable to her: that is, she had chosen as her dwelling place the wounded side of Jesus Christ, finding there in His pierced Heart the source of her love for God and other people.

The Sienese virgin was one of the first saints to whom it pleased Jesus to reveal the secrets of His divine Heart. The feet of Christ, nailed to the Cross, were for Catherine the first rung of the ladder that led to His side where He manifested the secrets of His Heart. In a letter to her disciples she exhorts them thus: "With feet of love we must climb up to the love of Jesus Crucified. In His side inflamed with love He shows us the secrets of His Heart... Truly, He is the fountain of living water and with great sweetness of love invites us...".

There are several splendid pages in her writings about the necessary dispositions for receiving the benefits of the heavenly food and, in particular, on the necessary purity of the ministers of God for celebrating the Holy Sacrifice. "The very angels, she says, should purify themselves for such a mystery, if it were possible that their nature could be so purified". For this reason Catherine wanted deep reverence to be shown to the ministers of God, even if they were unworthy of it, and rebuked everyone who did not give all due respect to their priestly dignity. To the rulers of Florence, who had rebelled against the common Father of all the faithful she tries to explain how hurtful it was for them "to deprive themselves of that dilection for which the Divine Son gives himself as food and calls us to a covenant of peace. Whoever does not obey Christ in this world cannot participate in the benefits of the blood of the Son of God, for He holds the key to that blood, and God has decided to grant us this blood only through His hands". We owe, therefore, immense respect to Pastors and Priests "because even if they were act like devils incarnate, we owe it not simply for what they in fact are, but out of obedience to Christ whose blood they administer".

Daily communion in those days was very unusual; and some people dared to reprove Catherine because she received the Holy Eucharist every day, quoting St. Augustine who neither praised nor criticized such a practice. To which she replied: "If St. Augustine does not disapprove of it, why sir, do you? While you ally yourselves to him, he opposes you".

She ceaselessly counseled everybody to keep their hearts pure in order to receive more abundantly the grace of the Blessed Sacrament; but the simple excuse of being unworthy in a very general sense was not, according to her way of thinking a good enough reason for abstaining from the Eucharist. To the famous painter Andrea Vanni who was also her disciple, she once wrote that Holy Communion must never be neglected neither by the devout nor by sinner under the pretext of unworthiness. "If a sinner is not well-disposed, he must become so; if one is a pious Christian, he must not abstain out of humility saying: I am not worthy of such a great gift, only when I am ready shall I receive it. One must never act thus, one must never think that one can become really worthy; and if one were to become worthy, he would still remain unworthy, cloaking pride with humility". Speaking again on the same subject, Catherine once cried out: "Oh foolish humility, and does He not see that you are unworthy? Do not delay, for you shall be no worthier of it at the end than at the beginning; notwithstanding all our efforts, we shall never be worthy of it".

So Catherine, who nourished herself totally on this celestial food, who sought to attract her spiritual children towards it, who was the pioneer of all the future eucharistic awakenings, showed herself to be a true daughter of St. Dominic, who was himself one of the greatest lovers of the Holy Eucharist and who always celebrated Mass with tears streaming down his face; and a true sister of St. Thomas Aquinas, who was the great theologian and poet of the Divine Sacrament and merited the title of "The Eucharistic Doctor".

THE DISCIPLES

Many people were attracted to a life of more intimate union with God thanks to Catherine; not only the other tertiaries and pious women generally, but also men of various ages and conditions, were influenced by her words, examples and writings. Most of them were children of the times; some came from illustrious families, passionate lovers of the things of this world who were saved by Catherine just at the edge of the abyss in which they were about to fall. With her help their hearts became gradually inflamed with love for spiritual things and, under her patient and loving tutelage, they progressed greatly in the ways of virtue and, quite a few, entered the religious life. They repaid her efforts with deep affection and close tenderness, sanctified and elevated by grace even though, in many cases, such attachments began as merely a vague liking for Catherine due to her moral superiority.

In this way she was able to wield a very special maternity with all the instincts and tenderness of a real mother. All these generous children which she called dearest ones in Christ accompanied Catherine on all her journeys and shared all her hardships; and they loved being with her. She encouraged them to travel along the arduous ways of sacrifice and exercised such a sweet dominion over them as very few saints have done with their followers in the history of the Church.

They could not help loving Christ Crucified in Catherine for she was a living image of Him. For the whole of her brief life, while she was literally tormented and consumed by the love of God, she also felt deeply for them according to the words of St. Paul: "Every day I labour to give birth in the presence of God". She wanted all her sons and daughters to be intimately united to God with words of love; and like a mother-eagle that almost forces her young to learn how to fly, Catherine incited them to renounce the things of this world and dedicate themselves to God. In fact, her efforts were so successful, that the love of God triumphed over all else in their hearts and they realized that they had been born anew. Society mocked them and nicknamed them "Catherinites"; but they could not have cared less.

These bright young people soon became ready to act as Catherine's closest collaborators in the new task for which God had destined her and His earthly vicar. Some of them, particularly Stefano Maconi, had already rendered important services to her, and she had always found in them an incomparable docility; but now their assistance was going to be required as never before and their childlike devotion to her, whom they called "mama", was going to be tested in the crucible.

Little more than a year of life remained to Catherine and it was a year of intense hard work for the good of a troubled, uncertain Church and an Italy threatened by new unsuspected dangers; it was also, for Catherine, a year of indescribable sorrows. It must have been a profoundly moving and remarkable sight: Catherine at work, surrounded by a brave band of gallant youths who, under her generalship, with true religious spirit, were dedicating themselves like armoured knights, for the triumph of the cause that lay closest to her heart, the welfare of the Church and the defence of the Vicar of Christ.

The young people of our own day who declare themselves able and willing to do the same work for the Church and the Supreme Pontiff, even if it costs blood, sweat and tears, will never find a better and more inspiring "General".

ROME

The Pope who succeeded Gregory XI, Urban VI, ex-Archibishop of Bari, was a man of austere virtue, animated by a lively desire to reform the decadent moral life of the clergy. Catherine was not unknown to him and he was fully aware of how unstintingly she had helped his predecessor in his difficult moments, almost injecting her own energy into his own veins.

He was so desirious of having her near him that he sent Blessed Raymond to persuade her to come to Rome. Catherine replied that she was willing to come, but wanted Raymond to bring a written request to that effect from the Pope in order to avoid the usual "gossip"; meanwhile she prepared for departure.

Catherine saw quite clearly that, once again, she had been chosen to enter the field and participate in a fierce struggle; and writing to Urban in humbly accepting his invitation she told him: "I wish that I was already in the midst of battle, suffering and fighting for you even unto death". In another letter, written to her dear spiritual daughter, Sister Danielle, who had received the Dominican habit at Orvieto, she said: "The time for weeping is at hand. Cease not to pray for the Vicar of Christ, that he may be granted light and strength to resist the blows of the incarnate demons, lovers only of themselves, who want to contaminate our Faith".

Catherine was right in shedding tears for the new calamity that had struck the Church. Those same cardinals who had elected the Pontiff and had rendered him the usual official homage and had asked him special favours, were now rebelling against him when they saw that he was in deadly earnest about uprooting vices and weeding out abuses in the Church. "As soon as he began to irk them – wrote the Saint – they immediately lifted up their heads". They met together at Tondi on September 18, 1378 and, with the full support of the local nobleman Count Gaetani, elected as anti-Pope Cardinal Robert of Genevra, who took the name Clement VII. He was the same man who as commander of the Bretons sent into Italy a few years back against Catherine's advice, had devastated the region of Romagna and allowed his soldiers to commit horrific massacres, especially during the siege of Cesena.

There was never any doubt about the legitimacy of Urban's election. On Easter Sunday, which fell on April 18 that year, of the twenty-three cardinals who made up the Sacred College, sixteen had performed the formal act of obedience in St. Peter's Basilica in Rome; the other six who had remained in Avignon shortly afterwards did likewise and even raised the Papal banner high above the walls of the castle. So the election of the anti-Pope was open rebellion, totally unjustified.

Catherine, once again, had her work cut out for her; and trusting fully in God, left her beloved Siena towards the middle of November, intuiting perhaps that she would never return, and arrived in Rome on the twenty-eight of the same month. Various other Mantellate went with her, Alessia Saracini, Francesca Gori, Lisa Colombini and Giovanna di Capo; some priests, the Dominican Bartolomeo Dominici, the hermit Fra Santi, the Augustinian Giovanni Tantucci; and three young men who acted as her secretaries, Barduccio Canigiani, Neri di Landoccio and Gabriele Piccolomini. After having stayed in a few different places here and there in the city, they finally took a house in Via del Papa, known today as Via Santa Chiara, that belonged to a certain Paola del Ferro. This house was used quite often as a sort of hotel by Sienese pilgrims.

Catherine did not waste a minute in presenting herself to the Pope, who received her with great joy and deep respect in the company of several cardinals and, after having heard her speak, exclaimed: "It is not this woman who speaks, but the Holy Spirit who speaks through her". And while they were all thinking of their own fates because of the worsening of the schism, they exclaimed: "This little lady confounds us! We are afraid and she is fearless".

In fact, the rebels had seized the Castle of Saint Angelo and the Pope was considering abandoning the Vatican and withdrawing to Santa Maria in Trastevere. The political intrigues, the misunderstanding and, above all, the wicked operations of Urban's enemies, had gained for the anti-Pope the explicit support of almost the whole of France, the Savoy and some of the Piemonte and Naples, which was split into two factions, one in favour of and the other against the legitimate Pope, including the Queen Joan, who bitterly opposed Urban.

Thus, Catherine was perfectly right when she previously insisted on peace at any price between the

Papacy and Florence back in the days of Gregory XI. The powerful position that Florence had obtained, the alliance she had with Milan, the wide influence she wielded over all Italy, expecially in Tuscany, all contributed to the fact that if, at the beginning of the schism, Florence were to actively assist the anti-Pope, the whole of Italy would be plagued into a deplorable betrayal.

Catherine, therefore was the instrument chosen by God to keep her country from religious and political ruin.

THE PRAYER CRUSADE

The Great Schism caused Catherine such piercing sorrow that the mere thought of it was enough to break her heart. She had always feared such an event and had written: "Any other evil, compared to this one, is like straw or a shadow: just thinking about it makes one tremble!". This is why, in accepting the Pope's call to come to Rome, she threw herself heart and soul into the struggle showing a contagious energy that touched Urban himself. "Come now, be fearless – she told him – participate in this battle!".

Certainly, the greatest weapon she possessed was her humble and fervent prayer, to which she added mortifications and vigils, reducing herself in the process to extreme bodily weakness. But if the flesh was weak, the spirit was ready and vigorous. Catherine was in constant agony. "Sometimes, the pain is simply too much for me to bear... Normal sweat is not enough to satisfy the holy and ardent desire I feel... I want to sweat blood!".

The letters and prayers that poured forth from Catherine's lips during this last period of her life are full of such ideas. She dictate them standing upright, with a loud voice and often in ecstasy, especially after Holy Communion. She would burst forth in acts of thanksgiving and love, expressing her desire that all hearts might be filled with the fire of love. The Sienese virgin prayed for the Church, asking God to free Her form the hands of the Devil, and to grant Her strength and victory against all enemies; and she prayed for the Supreme Pontiff asking God to give him a manly heart. "I will never cease – she told her God – knocking at the door of your mercy my beloved, until you exalt him, until you make him burn with bold desire, so that with benignity, charity, purity and wisdom he may proceed in all his acts, and drag the whole world to himself". She prayed for the cardinals, that instead of becoming superfluous and sterile branches in the Church, they might produce fruit with the examples of their own virtuous lives; and even for her adversaries, she prayed that their hardness of heart might be softened and she offered herself as a victim-soul saying: "Punish their sins in me. Behold my body, let it become the anvil for them, so that their sins may be expiated". And with singular affection, Catherine addressed the Blessed Virgin Mary, "temple of the Trinity, bearer of fire and of mercy, producer of fruit, giver of peace, fructiferous soil from which we receive the fragrant flower of the only-begotton Word of God, chariot of fire that brought to us the fire which was hidden under the ashes of His humanity". To Our Lady, she entrusted the sweet bride of her most sweet Son, and His Vicar on earth and His entire people. Catherine also prayed, especially, for her own spiritual children, that they might become "inflamed coals, burning with love for God and neighbour".

This was the Crusade proclaimed by Catherine for the benefit of the Church at that terrible moment. During Lent of that 1379, she practised the Way of the Stations. According to an ancient custom beginning on Ash Wednesday, the pious faithful in Rome would every day visit various fixed churches that were famous for their relics of martyrs in order to obtain the

Holy Indulgences. In that year Catherine tried to gather all her followers and bring them with her on these visits for the edification of everybody, thus invigourating more and more the powers of her soul with the remembrance of those champions of the faith. Tired and pained as she was, Catherine never complained while she made her daily rounds, leaning for support, more often than not, on the arm of her dear Barduccio and raising her eyes to heaven. She even visited the Vatican Basilica everyday; and, near the Confession of St. Peter she would remain for hours, often in ecstasy. "When it is the third hour – mid-morning, we should say, she wrote to Blessed Raymond – and I get up from the table, you will see a corpse walking towards St. Peter's, and there I shall stay until the hour of vespers". She prayed to the great Apostle asking him to defend his successor against the power of hell.

Catherine requested prayers from those who were far away: she remembered, above all, her dear Company of the Virgin, located in Siena, which was a centre of religious fervour. Many of her disciples who had remained behind gathered together there and, in her absence, called themselves "the lost sheep". This pious society supported the real Pope, and the zeal with which they did so rapidly extended to the entire city. When the anti-Pope's ambassador, Alderigo Albertinelli, announced his arrival, the whole populace responded that it was ready to stone him to death in the streets if he dared enter the city; so he decided not to make his visit. Catherine herself seemed to be working in those fervent disciples, encouraging and stimulating them to remain solid in their obedience to the Vicar of Christ.

To everyone she addressed her message of prayer, to those near, to those distant, to religious and to lay people. "Cease not to pray for the Holy Church", she urged her sons and daughters in Siena, "and for our Lord Pope Urban VI, for it is most necessary to do so... By means of the prayers and the loving anxious desires of his servants, God will grant mercy to the world. Sons and daughters, tell everybody that now is the time to weep to pray and to sigh for the sweet bride of Christ and for the entire Christian people so heavily afflicted by its own sins".

It is simply astonishing to see how many hardships Catherine took upon herself, adding them to all her prayers and pains of expiation. In these last months of her life, she rose above all her contemporaries and, rather than acting in a mild-mannered way, dominated them. She thought out a defence plan that consisted in two great actions: to sustain with all her strength the legitimate election of Urban VI, and maintain in total union with him all the dispersed members of the Church, including Italy. History attests that this humble woman made the most valid contribution to the worthy cause at that moment.

What we must really admire in her is not the daughter of the dyer of Fontebranda, but a miracle of God. The Pope was not deceiving himself when he said that in Catherine he had found "a divine help".

FOR THE UNITY OF THE CHURCH

The powerful love that Catherine had for the Church of Jesus Christ made her consider any attach against its unity as a great crime and a true work of diabolical perfidiousness. Whoever separated himself from this unity was for Catherine a putrid member, excluded from participating in the Blood, deprived of the divine lymph that flows in every part of the mystical body of Christ. Thus she approved of any means available in order to spare the Church from such a disaster, even if it meant giving her own life. This was a holy and noble desire on Catherine's part against all those degenerate sons of the Church, who with their petty ambitions and cowardly fears were trying to break the bonds that bound them to the Common Father.

Together with her prayers and penances, Catherine made immense efforts to win over many secular rulers to the cause of Urban VI. She turned to the King of Hungary and Poland, Louis the Great, telling him to make peace with Venice, and to obey Pope Urban who had also asked him for assistance, "because those who should have been the pillars and defenders of the holy faith have abandoned it and become blind and leaders of the blind". The King, who knew their lies, ought to always protect the Holy Church against heretics and false Christian: "And will you sit back and allow the anti-Christ, a follower of the Devil, and a certain female [the Queen of Naples n.d.t.] to touch our faith in order only to ruin it and throw it into darkness and confusion? Have pity on our Father, Pope Urban VI. Truly, he should seek comfort in God alone and place all faith and hope in Him. But he also hopes that God will persuade you to share this burden for His honour and the good of the Holy Church".

To Charles of Durazzo, called Charles of the Peace, Catherine sent a letter by means of Martin of Taranto, one of the Pope's Chamberlains, asking him for help against the rebels, who "having renounced their sonship, had become slaves of the Devil, of the world and of the flesh. Be a valiant knight: after having won the interior battle in your soul, take part in the external battle and, as a pillar of the Church, come to her assistance. How shameful and unpleasant in the sight of God to see so much coldness in the hearts of the lords of this would who have only words to offer to this most sweet Bride".

Catherine probably wrote a letter to Richard II, King of England, which unfortunately has been lost. In order to keep the English under obedience to Urban and convince them to use their influence on the other nations of Europe, she sought the services of William Flete, the celebrated English hermit who did continue to work for the noble cause even after the death of Catherine.

To the King of France, Charles V of Anjou, who had allowed himself to be dragged to the side of the anti-Pope, she wrote: "I am rather surprised that a Catholic man who wants to be brave and God-fearing should permit himself to be led astray like a small boy and not notice the ruin he is causing for himself and others". And if he still had any doubts, he ought to consult the doctors at the Sorbonne. "You have the fountain of all knowledge there", she told him; and, in fact, the famous University had declared itself in favour of Urban, but then changed its opinion because of political intrigues.

In order to keep Italy in Urban's camp, Catherine spoke to all those who had some authority in the major Italian cities, admonishing them to provide for the defence of the Church and the good of the nation. Florence, which had resumed friendly relations with the Pope, now energetically sustained him. And Catherine, who had suffered and worked so much to obtain that peace, wrote to the Gonfaloniere of Justice and the Priors of the Arts telling them to quickly eliminate the seeds of discord from their city because, "nothing weakens States so much as internal divisions. Urban VI, true High Pontiff and Vicar of Christ on earth, has forgiven you with great charity, treating you as though you had never even offended him. Be grateful and respectful! Because gratitude is that virtue which nurtures piety and it invites God Himself to increase and multiply His graces".

She repeated the same message to the Rectors of Perugia: "If we do not help our father, we shall be in great danger, because we shall place ourselves outside the fortress and become weak. The arm of the Holy Church has not been broken: and from its momentary atrophy it will be strengthened as well as all those who trust in it. God will be wrathful and will punish us if we do not assist our Pope Urban VI and our faith. Forgive me, but the necessities of the Holy Church and your own salvation force me to speak thus".

And she thought particularly of her own Siena. To it she sent the very learned Augustinian Cardinal

Bonaventura Baduario of Padua, who preached in the Cathedral on Pope Urban's legitimacy; and, later on, she even urged her fellow-Sienese to send not only money but arms to help the Pontiff. If anyone refused to lend a hand because of the personal failings of Urban, she said: "He is really a good, virtuous, God-fearing man who acts with right and holy intentions as nobody else has done for a long time in the Church of God; and anyway, whether or not he is a good or a bad man, reverence is owed to him not only for what he is in himself but for the blood of Christ and for the dignity and authority of God who has given him to us. This authority and dignity is not diminished for any defect he may have, nor does his ministry lose any of its power; our reverence and obedience towards him must never diminish".

Venice remained in union with the Pontiff thanks to Catherine, who, writing to the Bishop, Angelo Corario, later Pope Gregory XII, wanted him to openly declare for Pope Urban VI, and wanted the city of lagoons to resist the pressures of the anti-Pope and his representatives: "Be the master of this city and bravely proclaim the truth abut the Pope Urban VI the true High Pontiff; and do your best to keep all the citizens in the faith, reverence and obedience they owe to the Holy Church and to His Holiness".

Catherine also looked for help among professional soldiers such as Count Alberigo of Belbiano, head of the famous Company of St. George, consisting of four-thousand infantry and four-thousand cavalry. She exhorted him to fight for Urban's cause while regreting the sad fact that she could do nothing but pray.

"We shall do what Moses did; when the people fought Moses prayed, and while he was praying, the people won". The great Captain, in fact, came to Rome, defeated the forces of the anti-Pope and, on April 29, captured the Castle of Sant'Angelo which they had been holding; the rulers of Rome offered Alberigo the keys to the Castle and, thanks to his victory, the Pope was able to leave Santa Maria in Trastevere and return safely to St. Peter's Basilica. The Pope never thought to make such a triumphant re-entry; he went barefoot, as in a penitential procession and was praised by Catherine who, writing to the seven Councillors of Rome and urging them to be grateful to God, said: "The example has been given by our Father, Pope Urban VI with which he thanks God for His graces, humbling himself and performing what has not been done for a very long time, going on procession barefoot. As sons and daughters, let us follow the tracks of our Father and thank God for His graces".

Catherine wanted them to also thank the military Company which had done so much to help them; and with a mother's heart, she thought of the "poor wounded" left over after the battle and sought help for them in all their needs. She also wanted the Romans to be grateful to the Keeper of the Castle, John Cenci, who with care and loyalty, a pure heart and great prudence assisted them in liberating the imposing fortress.

Writing about it all to Urban himself, she expressed her joy thus: "I am happy, holy Father, and my heart is uplifted, for my eyes have seen the will of God accomplished in you…, namely in that humble action, not performed in ages, of the holy procession. Oh, how pleasing it must have been to God". Catherine thanked the Virgin Mary and the glorious Apostle Peter, to whom she was deeply devoted: "I rejoice in this sweetest Mother, Mary and in Peter, Prince of the Apostles, who have restored you to your place...".

And even if the hateful schism did not end immediately because of the obstinacy of the anti-papal party, the efforts of this humble woman to save the Church from total destruction will always arouse admiration. She was also the perfect instrument of God to keep her own nation, Italy, faithful to the true successor of Peter at the moment in which its defection from the Church seemed inevitable.

AGAIINST THE ARMIES OF THE EVIL ONE

It is difficult to summarize, even briefly, the many phases of the struggle carried on by Catherine in Rome in 1379 and during the first months of 1380, by the side of the Pontiff against those who, denying the legitimacy of his election and trying to drag along to their party all of Christendom, appeared to her eyes as "the armies of the evil one against Christ on earth". If history had not left us a most faithful record of it all and if the most reliable witnesses had not testified to the absolute truth of the facts, it would be unbelievable that such a humble woman should had dared and obtained so much. It must have been amazing to see her, exhausted and consumed by tears and by the sorrow she carried in her heart. Her life seemed to hang on the thinnest of threads, but under that tenuous thread lay hidden the soul of a giantess, who fought with indomitable courage as long as God sustained her, refused to listen to voices of human prudence, did not surrender in front of difficulties, and did not mitigate the vigour of her zeal; a true victim of love who defended at all costs the violated honour of her Groom, whose real living image she saw in the Roman Pontiff. The letters through which up to that moment she had carried on her singular apostolate and in which she tried to inflame other hearts with fire of divine love, by destroying the roots of hate and discord, became more than ever before mighty weapons, fiery arrows against all kinds of enemies to awaken their conscience and induce them to change their ways. Francesco Malavolti, one of her secretaries in Rome, has described Catherine's method of dictating. Very often she would have three secretaries simultaneously at her disposal and she would begin speaking without interruption on various topics, addressing her words now to one, now to another, smoothly directing the verbal flow and flawlessly picking up an argument exactly where she had previously left off. She would fix her gaze heavenwards, fold her arms, hide her face in her hands and her speech was sometimes punctured by groans and weeping.

The well-known and ferocious letter that Catherine wrote to the three Italian cardinals, Pietro Corsini of Florence, Giacomo Orsini of Rome and Simone Borzan of Milan who, after having elected and supported Urban vilely abandoned him, belongs to the first months of 1379. "You wish to persuade us that you elected Urban out of fear! Whoever says this lies in his throat. I am not obliged to speak to you with respect, because you do not deserve any respect!". She calls them "blind and stupid" and tries to make them reflect on the dastardliness into which they had fallen by separating themselves from the head of the body. They are no longer flowers that emanate pleasant odours, lights shining brightly from on high, angels who fight for us against the hellish enemy, but exactly the opposite. They have become cruel children towards the mother who has nourished them at her breast and have deserved a thousand deaths.

She regrets the fact that they are not there in front of her, because if they were, who would "sting them with her living voice". And, in Catherine's opinion, being Italians, their fault was even more serious.

"Humanly speaking, Christ on earth is an Italian, and you are Italians and yet you have no love for your country like the ultramontanes". If she could not thus rebuke foreigners, she could assuredly rebuke those three for being traitors to their own country. She ends the letter with a hope for their conversion and expressed the desire to see them "bathed in the blood of the Lamb shed for us with fiery love and restored to the bosom of the Father".

No less severe were the reprimands which Catherine launched against Count Onorato Gaetani of Fondi who, having previously been loyal to the Church, was now playing the host to those rebellious cardinals who had elected the anti-Pope in his city.

She begins by calling him "most dear Father", but then attacks him at once for having consigned himself over to the "tyrannical whim of self-love", thus changing the garden of his soul into a dark forest. "In your heart of hearts, she says, you believe that Urban VI is the one, true Pontiff. I knew that God has given you enough light to see the truth: but now your own egoism has made you deny it. For the love of God do not continue in this way! It is human to err; but it is diabolical to persist in error. Return to yourselves, for sin will not go unpunished, particularly when it is committed against the Holy Church. Leave your errors before it's too late; death comes soon and we don't even think about it and we shall find ourselves in the hands of the High Judge".

Catherine also crossed swords with one of the most corrupt women of their age: Joan, Queen of Naples. She was the daughter of the Count of Anjou, called

Lackland by the Italians, nephew to Philip the Fair. Catherine had once already written to and exhorted Joan, because of her title as Queen of Jerusalem, to be a faithful servant of the Holy Church; but when the rebellion broke out against the legitimate Pope, Joan passed over to the French party and, it was said, lent a helping hand in the election of the anti-Pope.

"From what they say – wrote Catherine – he was elected with the help of your arm". And she begged her "to turn back. For if you do not, you will be seen for what you really are, an unstable woman. Eliminate the poison from your soul and then my soul shall rejoice to see the fruit of your obedience, for I care deeply about your salvation. I only wish I could do more than just write words against those who plant heresy in the mystical body of the Holy Church".

Catherine would have liked to go to Naples herself and talk to the mis-informed Queen, but the Pope would not hear of it. She satisfied her desire by sending her dear disciple Neri di Landoccio to accompany the Abbot Lisolo Brancacci, chosen by the Pope, with some letters for several influential people. She even wrote another letter to the same Queen, always hoping for a change of mind on her part. "I have noticed a great change in your person for which I can no longer call you mother, because you have become the slave of the Devil who is the father of all lies… You are already dead spiritually and you shall be so even bodily if you do not desist".

Catherine also had a few more things to say about the anti-Pope whom Joan defended, revealing the cunning and double-dealing of his electors: "Where is this right man they have elected as anti-Pope? What kind of man have they really chosen? A holy man? By no means, but a wicked man, a demon, for he acts like one. The real demon tries to hide from the truth and this fellow does the same. And why did they not choose the right man? Because they knew perfectly well that the "right" man would have preferred death rather than accept their election!".

She stoutly denied the charge that her own mind was unclear and turned it against the Queen whose own passions had obscured the light of truth. And she closes, admonishing Joan once again to convert "in order to void the rod, to remember death, to give no thought to riches, status, dignity, nobility or people, for nothing and nobody will be able to save her from the Tribunal of Christ the Judge!… With heartfelt sorrow, I tell you this, for I tenderly love your salvation".

Unfortunately, the ambitious Queen did not desist from her unhappy rebellion, though the Neopolitans themselves and their Archbishop kept the faith by supporting Urban VI. Joan even reached the point of trying to capture and imprison the Pontiff and slay his closest adherents, sending a certain Rinaldo of the Orsini to accomplish it all, and she invited the anti-Pope to Naples offering him one of her castles. That beautiful city thus became the rock of the anti-Christ against the Roman See.

THE FAREWELL TO THE FATHER

Catherine was so occupied in protecting the interests of the Church, that she had hardly any time to think about herself; she lived only for its cause, struggling with God by means of prayers, tears, groans and with men by uprooting from their hearts pride and cupidity, the real causes of all those terrible discords.

The best proof that she did not think of herself was her willingness to be deprived of her only earthly comfort. Blessed Raymond of Capua had been her spiritual director and she was keenly aware of her need for his wise and loving support. And yet Catherine herself more than once advised him to leave her in order to better serve the interests of the Church wherever necessary. For example, in that year 1379, Raymond went to Naples to speak to Queen Joan. As we know, Catherine would have liked to have gone there, but since at that very moment St. Catherine of Sweden, daughter of St. Brigette, who was aquainted with the Queen of Naples, was in Rome, the Pontiff desired both Catherines to go together. The Swedish Princess, however, had valid reason for excusing herself from such a mission and Raymond dissuaded the Pope from sending two virtuous young women to that corrupt court. When the Sienese Catherine got wind of it, she let Raymond have a piece of her mind: "If Catherine [of Alexandria n.d.t.], Margaret, Agnes and the other holy virgins had been held back by such cowardliness, they would never have won the crown of martyrdom! Do not all good virgins have a Spouse who can defend them from wicked men?". Raymond

spies of Queen Joan who set traps for the unwary and once captured one of Raymond's travelling companions. They were in some danger of death and on the advice of another of his confreres, Raymond decided to turn back. The legation to France thus came to an unexpected halt and Raymond tried to continue in Genoa his mission of defending the Church with even more zeal after having been elected shortly afterwards Provincial of the Dominicians in Lombardy and, then, Master General of the whole Order. But Catherine, with her uncontrollable enthusiasm saw only weakness in Raymond's decision to turn back even if he had run the risk of being murdered and she sent him a bittersweet reproof: "You were not fit to enter the fray! And like a little boy you have been tossed out of it. My naughty little father, how beautiful our souls might have become, if with your blood you had cemented a rock in the edifice of the Holy Church for the love of Jesus! Let us leave behind such childish fears, and like a grown man, let us run back to the battle field… drown yourself in the blood of Christ crucified, and bathe yourself in that blood, console yourself in it, exult in it, grow and fortify yourself in it and fly as a brave knight to seek the honour of God and the good of the Holy Church". In another letter she tells him that before his return, she will receive a wonderful grace, for she will leave this world. He instead shall remain. And she says with all honesty that he is not yet ready to give his life for Christ. Therefore, he must continue working without fear or weakness: "If you are a man in your promises, do not be womanish when the nail is hammered into you, for I would have you remember Christ crucified and Mary. Be a man, always!". Raymond never saw Catherine again, but her words and examples, were, for the rest of his life, the greatest stimulus he could have wished for in his work for the good of the Church and, particularly, in his call to the whole Dominican Family, which he governed for twenty years, to return to its primitive fervour.

THE APPEAL TO THE DISCIPLES

In the struggles that Catherine gallantly undertook to keep as many people as possible faithful and obedient to the true Pope and to expose the wily schemes of the schismatics, she sought help from all her children. Like a captain who gathers his best men around him in the hour of greatest danger, so she wanted to have her disciples around her in Rome, especially her fellow-Sienese who had assisted her so loyally in various other tasks. She attracted them with the love of a sister and mother; and though they were far away from her, they were always with her in their hears and thoughts, hoping that she would not collapse under the strain of work. Catherine's three faithful secretaries were already with her in Rome along with some of her other daughters, Lisa, Alessia, Cecca and Giovanna di Capo. Stefano Maconi had to remain in Siena because of some family problems; perhaps his mother, Monna Giovanna, knowing and worrying about how impulsive and independent he was, wanted to keep him at home under her watchful eye. Among the Dominican religious, Fra Bartolomew Dominici, who had accompanied Catherine to Rome, was now back in Siena as Prior of San Domenico, and Blessed Raymond, as we have seen, had already left her forever. The invitation she sent to these dearest friends to come to Rome and fight and suffer with her are deeply moving. To Stefano especially, Catherine sent many affectionate letters; and Barduccio, who usually wrote most of these for her, privately added some of his own sentiments in them. To Stefano and to all the members of the Company of the Virgin Mary, she said with firm hope: "If you become what you must become, you will set all Italy on fire!". And even while, with jocular intimacy, she calls Stefano an "unworthy and ungrateful little son" she says to him: "I want you to act like a man. The blood of many glorious martyrs buried here in Rome, who with so much fire of love gave their blood and lives for love of Life is boiling and inviting you and the others to come and fight for the glory and praise of God's name and of the Holy Church". Stefano had previously asked Catherine to obtain certain indulgences, as usual, from the Holy Father personally, for himself and some others; but for once, in order to arouse him to come, she thus replied: "About those indulgences you asked me to procure for you, let me tell you not to expect them or anything else from me, if you don't come here yourself to get them...". She repeated the same invitation to others, including a certain Peter di Giovanni Ventura: "Let me see if you really want to leave home and come here. If you do, hurry up and finish whatever you still have to do...". Many religious belonging to various Orders, holy men all of them, had become disciples of the Saint; and, during last months of her life, she asked them to help her with their talents. To Don Giovanni delle Celle, a monk at Vallombrosa, she wrote: "Necessity calls us, duty impels us. Do you not see today, as never before, in the Holy Church, how necessary it is for all her children, nourished at her breast, to rise up and help her and the Father?". And she wants him "to enter the battle with a manly heart" and if need be, to give his life. "Now is the hour for all the servants of God to come forth and work". For all those who might complain about so many religious going to Rome, she has a ready answer: "You are not coming here in order to obtain prelacies, but to work; the dignity that you seek consists in sweat, tears, vigils and continual prayers!". Catherine turned to even the more strictly enclosed monks, such as the Carthusians, manifesting the Pope's desire "to have the servants of God at his side". To Don Bartholomew Serafini, prior of Gorgona, she made a special plea and sent him a list of the monks that he should send: "Do this as quickly as you can and do not waste time for the Church of God has no need of slackers. Put aside all other projects even if they are important, and order the ones whose names are on the list to come here at once. Do not hesitate, please, for the love of God; come and work in this garden!". So the good Father Serafini did as Catherine wished bringing other confrères with him. Other people summoned by Catherine were the Dominican fra Leonardo of Montepulciano and the three hermits of Monte Luca near Spoleto, Fra Andrea of Lucca, Fra Naldo and Fra Lando. Here is how the Saint invited these three to leave their hermitage: "Stick your heads out and come and fight for the truth. You must not retire for any reason, neither for the hardships you might have to face nor for hunger, thirst, death or the desire to live quietly". Using the example of a dog that barks to wake up its master, she added: "For the infinite goodness and mercy of God has provided for the needs of the Holy Church by giving her a good and upright pastor, who wants to have around himself these dogs that bark for the love of God continuously, that are wide-awake and watchful, so that they may wake others... I beg you and order you to come here immediately and accomplish the will of God and of the Vicar of Christ, who gently calls you and the others". Even Andrea of Lucca, old and feeble as he was, exposed himself to the hazards of the journey and went to Rome. Catherine also sent urgent appeals to the Augustinian hermits of Lecceto. In that holy monastery, about three miles from Siena, there was among the other monks under the direction of the Master Giovanni Fantucci, an Englishman named William Flete, nicknamed the Bacelor, to whom the Saint wrote many letters. Flete lived in a cave deep in the nearby woods during the daylight hours and returned to the monastery in the evenings. Catherine had sometimes gone to visit him there and now she would have liked him to come to Rome; but Flete absolutely refused to leave his tranquil oasis. She judged him rather severely for this inopportune desire of peace and quiet, which was only a thinly disguised egoism on his part; and, writing to one of Flete's brother monks, Fra Antonio, Catherine cited the example of the great patron of all monks and hermits, St. Anthony of Tebaide, who though preferring to live in fervent solitude away cities, had no difficulty in travelling to Alexandria in order to defend persecuted Christians. This, she said, has always been the custom of the true servants of God, to come forward in times of necessity and adversity "leaving the solitary life for a short period does not damage the spirit. The spirit is weak in the worst way, if it loses itself simply because of a change of place. As if God were an acceptor of places and could he found only forests! Do not worry about leaving the woods: even here you will still be surrounded by them; come, do not hesitate, do not sleep now dearest sons: it is time to wake up". The needs of the Church occupied the first place in her thoughts and the unity of the Church was her main interest. The Master, Giovanni Fantucci and Fra Antonio obeyed her summons and went to Rome; William Flete obstinately remained in his woods. We must remark, however, that from his lonely hermitage he worked for the good of the Church, writing letters, to his friends in England and thus, keeping that nation firm in its obedience to the true Pope. For all this, Catherine, was the living personification of the Church in danger, waiting to be helped by the love and sacrifices of her children. She used to compare the Church to a ship and say that she was carrying it on her shoulders, feeling all its weight. And around her, fatigued and literally consumed by slow martyrdom, were gathered, thanks to God, her most loving sons and daughters.

THE DEATH OF CATHERINE

During these last few months of her life, news had been reaching Siena of Catherine's deteriorating state of health. She even had to stop her daily visits to St. Peter's Basilica where she used to go using a cane and leaning on the arm of her beloved Barduccio, remaining there until evening in prayer. As soon as she heard about Catherine's condition, her elderly mother, Lapa went down to Rome. We can well imagine her reaction when she saw her daughter lying on a miserable cot, totally exhausted, a shadow of what she once had been.

Barduccio who assisted Catherine continuously, spoke incessantly of the pains and hardships that afflicted her during the last months of 1380. "Notwithstanding that infirmity, she always applied herself to prayer, which to us seemed a miracle for the frequent humble sighs and bitter weeping that gushed forth from her heart". Everyday she received Holy Communion and, though weakened by atrocious pains, managed to raise her eyes to heaven with joy and say, "I thank you, eternal Spouse, that everyday you give me, your miserable servant, so many and such marvellous graces". Thus, she literally dragged herself along right up to the Sunday preceeding the Feast of the Ascension which turned out to be the last day of her life. In the meantime, another of her dearest and most beloved disciples arrived in Rome, Stefano Maconi. Catherine had written to him: "When you hear a voice calling, answer it". And behold, one night, he heard a loud clear voice crying: "Go, run to

Rome, for your mother is about to depart". He obeyed immediately. Catherine welcomed him with indescribable affection saying: "Finally you have come! Now go to confession, then come back to me and I shall let you know the divine will". Stefano obeyed, and when he returned to the bedside of his holy mother, who by now was unable to speak above a whisper, together with Baruccio Francesco Malavolti and other disciples, he heard from her lips her last testament of love: "My children, love each other always. So shall you be my joy and my crown". Then, calling them individually, Catherine advised one to retire to a hermitage, another to do works of charity in the world, another to become a priest; and when it was Stefano's turn, reaching out to touch him with her feeble hand, she said: "Stefano, I command you, in the name of God and in holy obedience, to enter the Carthusian Order. To this God is calling you". Up to that moment such a thought had never entered Stefano's head. But the will of his holy mother was to him the voice of God and he did as he was told; and the facts of history attest that he became an honour to the Carthusian Order by leading a most holy life. The venerable Abbot of St. Antimo was also present and, seeing that death was nigh, gave Catherine absolution and the last anointing. After this, everybody noticed that she began acting rather oddly, as though the Evil One was, for the last time, trying to tempt and disturb her. And she began to say: "I have sinned, Lord, have mercy on me", which she repeated sixty times, simultaneously raising her right arm each time and letting it fall upon the bed. Then, another sixty times, but without moving her arms or any other part of her body, she exclaimed: "Oh Holy God, have mercy on me". Catherine then began to say many other things, and with her head resting on the bosom of Alessia, who was sitting on the bed, almost breathless with groaning and weeping, she confessed the sins that she remembered having committed during life; when, suddenly, she appeared to be greatly distressed by something. She remained silent for a few minutes and, with as much force as she could muster in her voice, exclaimed: "Vainglory? No, never, but true glory in Christ Crucified". Catherine was undergoing the last assault of the Devil who, knowing how many good works she had accomplished in her life, was trying to suggest that she had done everything for her own selfish glory when, in truth, she had always given all the credit and honour to God. It was extremely touching to see poor, desolated Lapa standing next to the bed, asking her daughter's blessing, while she asked her mother for her blessing. Calling for the last time all her beloved sons and daughters around her, she said in a sure voice: "Know all of you that Urban VI is the true Pontiff and may none of you hesitate to die for him". She immediately lost consciousness. Shortly afterwards Catherine awoke and said: "You are calling me, oh Lord; I am coming to you, not thanks to my own merits, but only because of your mercy!". After another brief silence, she shouted: "Blood, blood, blood!". Lastly with hardly a thread of voice, she whispered: "Father, into your hands I entrust my soul and my spirit" Catherine looked up to heaven for a moment, then lowered her head and died. She was thirty-three years and thirty-five days of age. It was the twenty-ninth of April and the Church was celebrating the feast day of the Dominican, St Peter Martyr.

THE SORROW OF THE CHILDREN

For the entire afternoon and evening of that day, Catherine's devoted family, now cruelly orphaned, sighed and wept. They decided not to reveal her death to anyone outside, thinking that the news of it might arouse a tumult among the locals. The door to the house remained jealously closed, so that nobody could enter. Far into the night, in agreement with the Prior of the Dominicans at the Minerva, Catherine's corpse was transported secretly to their church by Stefano himself, wrapped in a simple sheet. The following morning, the Saint's virginal body was placed behind the gate of St. Dominic's Chapel where it was visited by people from all over Rome; it remained there for seven days during which many extraordinary healings and graces were obtained by invocations to her.

Meanwhile Lapa with Alessia and all the other dear disciples, holed up in their little house in Via del Papa, were completely disconsolate, bearing a great emptiness in their hearts. They did not weep for Catherine, though; they were all certain that she had already joined the blessed in heaven and was praying for them; but they were sad at feeling themselves orphans in the world, unsure about the future, deprived so soon of she who had been in every occasion their guide, not only in spiritual matters, but in all the circumstances of life, especially in the work they had begun for the love and defence of the Church to which Catherine had always urged them. Pope Urban VI expressed his deep sorrow for the death of Catherine who had been his finest supporter in his darkest hours; and he ordered a solemn funeral to be celebrated at the Minerva, at his own expense on May 2 with the entire clergy of the city present, while a second funeral celebration was held a few days later by order of Giovanni Cenci, Senator of Rome, as an act of homage by the whole populace. Another high-placed prelate who sincerely mourned Catherine's death was Tommaso Petra, Apostolic Pronotary and personal Secretary of the Pontiff; ever since the day he had met Catherine in Avignon he had felt a high esteem and profound veneration for her. Their friendship blossomed quickly and he assisted her in her last hours. And, naturally, we cannot fail to be moved by the poignant sorrow of the Saint's disciples, who, during those difficult first days, in their efforts to bravely bear up under the impact of her death, wrote consoling letters one to another. To the dear Barduccio, who must have keenly felt the pain of his loss, Giovanni delle Celle wrote: "How shall we live now that our mother, our joy, has left us? There is nothing we can do but weep hot tears over our misfortune. I know, the angels in heaven are celebrating a great feast in her honour, but I weep, for it is the sweetest thing for me to do". Neri di Landoccio was in Naples at the time and knew nothing as yet about Catherine's passing until Neri di Duccio wrote to him: "Know that our dearest and treasured mother has gone to heaven. I feel like an orphan, for all my comfort was in her and now I can't stop crying... I do not cry for her, but for myself, because I have lost the most precious thing on earth. We are all now like sheep without a shepherd". The most devastated of all was, undoubtedly, Stefano Maconi. After having done all he could for the dead Catherine, after having poured out torrents of tears and kisses on her closed coffin, he returned to Siena with a broken heart and in a state of uncontrollable mental anguish, for now he had nobody to guide him and he was uncertain of his future. He felt the need of disattaching himself totally from the world, as his holy mother had commanded him to do in her last moments; but for a while, he did not know where to go or how to do so and for days on end he just wandered aimlessly around the countryside near Siena. Some thought he had gone mad. Catherine's invisible hand was helping him, though. Hardly a year had passed when he received the religious habit in the Carthusan Monastery in Pontignano. The sufferings of Catherine's sons and daughters after her death was not sterile. They all remembered her in their hearts, her life and her dynamic love; and following her teachings and examples became in different ways, according to their individual preferences and conditions, humble instruments for the salvation of souls and the good of the Church.

CANONIZED

The extraordinary graces granted through the intercession of Catherine, especially to those who with faith visited her sacred remains in the Church of Santa Maria Minerva, or touched one of her relics, or simply invoked her name, were indeed innumerable and confirmed the title of Blessed and Saint which the whole Roman populace had already attributed to her. Catherine's fame spread rapidly, everyone wanted an image or some kind of remembrance of her, the letters and other writings were conserved like priceless treasures, the great biography composed by Blessed Raymond of Capua was eagerly awaited and read by all; and a substantial body of literature began to grow up around her, of whom other saints, Popes and illustrious personages sang praises. Catherine's remains soon received the honours usually reserved only to the Servants of God and, after three years of repose in a cypress coffin in the little cemetery attached to the Dominican Priory of the Minerva, was transported on October 3, 1383 into the Church and enclosed in a marble tomb by blessed Raymond, who was now Master General of the Dominican Order; and on that same occasion, in order to please her fellow citizens of Siena, he separated the head from the body and sent Fra Ambrose Sansedoni and Fra Tommaso della Fonte with it to them while one of Catherine's fingers was given to Stefano Maconi, On May 5, 1384, with a pomp never seen before in Siena, the sacred head was brought into the Church of San Domenico which became the most famous sanctuary of the Saint. The entire city participated in the magnificent spectacle; four hundred small girls dressed in white sang hymns and strew flowers while four Dominican religious carried the precious relic enclosed in a bust of gilded copper under a rich canopy. It must have been a most touching thing to see Lapa, Catherine's eighty year old mother walking in the procession, propped up by the good Alessia Saracini and to hear all the people call her blessed, while their holy strains wafted towards heaven. All the Saint's children showed up for the ceremony. The most conspicuous among them were Neri dei Pagliaresi, Neri di Landoccio, Barduccio Canigiani, Christopher di Gano, Francesco Malavolti, Gabriele Piccolomini and many others. And, at the head of them all stood Stefano Maconi who had rushed down to Siena from Pontignano in order to help the city Fathers and the Bishop organize the memorable event. The Sacred Head was greeted by an impressive host of Dominicans from all over Tuscany who gratefully guarded it in the Church of San Domenico. To another Domenican Saint, Antonio Pierozzi, prior of the Minerva in Rome and later, Archbishop of Florence, fell the happy task of erecting a most worthy resting place for his illustrious sister in St. Domenico. He commissioned the sculptor Isaiah of Pisa to build the actual urn with a little statue of the Saint next to it; the urn was then placed in the Chapel of the Rosary surrounded by angels holding various written praises in their hands. The official process of canonization, began in 1411 was, unhappily, suspended because of the Great Western Schism which continued to afflict the Church until the Council of Constance, during which the Pope Martin V was elected finally putting an end to it all. The overwhelming joy of elevating Catherine to the honours of the altar fell to a Sienese Pope, Pius II, formely known as Enea Silvio Piccolomini; and the solemn canonization took place on June 29, 1461, the feast day of the Holy Apostles Peter and Paul, in the Vatican Basilica. Some years later, the Pontiffs, Urban VIII and then, Benedict XII officially asserted the authenticity of the Stigmata that Catherine had received during her life and a special feast was granted to celebrate that event, particularly in the Dominican Order and the whole of Tuscany. Throughout the ensuing centuries many other honours have been bestowed upon St. Catherine; for example, several churches and altars erected in her name and in 1637 the transfer of the walls of the room in which she died to a tiny room behind the sacristy of the Minerva; and special mention must be made of the solemn homage paid in 1855, upon the completion of repairs done to that church, by the whole of Rome, when the body of St. Catherine was carried in stately magnificence through the streets of the city, and then placed once again in its urn under the main altar of the Minerva which had been consecrated by Pope Pius IX, who with a decree of April 13, 1866 declared St. Catherine "Co-Patroness" of Rome. Pope Pius XII, with his decree of June 18, 1939, proclaimed St. Catherine "Patroness of Italy", along with St. Francis of Assisi as Patron of the same. And, on October 4, 1970, Pope Paul VI officially declared St. Catherine of Siena "Doctor of the Church".

THE HOMAGE OF ART

The fine arts which flowered in their greatest splendour especially in Tuscany in the XIV century, did not neglect to pay their respects to St. Catherine. A most lifelike portrait was done just ten years after her death by one of her fervent disciples Andrea Vanni; originally part of a larger frescoe, it was disattached in 1667 and placed in the well-known Chapel of the Vaults in the Church of San Domenico where it may still be seen today above a small altar. After Catherine's death many artists diligently conserved her effigy and reproduced her in paintings and frescoes, now by herself, now next to the Virgin Mary and other saints, or in some episode of her life, particularly the Mystical Marriage with Jesus, or when she was imprinted with the Sacred Stigmata. Unfortunately, several other portraits have been lost during the centuries even though Blessed Raymond ordered then to be painted in so many churches belonging to the Order. The custom of portraying Catherine with St. Dominic began quite early; later on other saints were sometimes added, especially our Lady in the act of giving both the holy rosary. Many of these works were true masterpieces, one of the most celebrated being that of Sassoferrata which is now in the Church of Santa Sabina in Rome. But more than enough works have survived to demonstrate the enthusiasm above all of the Sienese, in glorifying with gentle and attractive colours their great Saint, even before Pius II canonized her. They painted Catherine not only in the churches and smaller oratories, but also in the hospitals, in their homes and in their very own town Hall; and they particularly loved to represent Catherine on the lids of coffins in order to place their dear deceased under her protection, always showing her in a most virginal pose with a lily in one hand and a book in the other. They often painted her in the company of the great Saint Bernardino canonized in 1450. The most famous portraitists of Catherine have belonged to the Sienese school: Giovanni di Paolo, Sano di Pietro, Lorenzo the Vecchietta, Francesco di Giorgio, Neroccio di Lando, Girolamo of Pecchia, Balducci, and towering above then all, Antonio de Bazzi, nicknamed Sodoma who was so struck by the spiritual beauty of the great woman, that he portrayed her in three sublime frescoes which are considered to be the best works produced by his brush. These three still admirably adorn the chapel where, just above the marble altar exquisitely sculptured by Giovanni di Stefano, is kept the treasure of the Sacred Head of Catherine. The three frescoes represent the stigmatization of the Saint, one of her ecstasies in which an angel offers her the Host and the tragic beheading of the callow youth from Perugia, Nicola di Tuldo, whose soul was seen by Catherine as it flew to heaven. Francesco Vanni covered the other wall of the Chapel with the frescoe of the liberation of a possessed woman and, under the archways he painted the two first biographers of Catherine, Raymond of Capua and Tommaso Caffarini. The house where the angelic little girl was born and raised, her father's shop and the small orchard were all transformed by the art of the Cinquecento, and became one of the most holy shrines in Siena, full of rich artistic memorials, affectionately guarded and constantly refurbished. Only one hundred years ago Alessandro Franchi painted with much finesse and rare piety the tiny austere bedroom which had been the scene of so many prodigies performed by God in the Sienese Virgin. The same homage was repeàted in various places: for example the Priory of Fiesole, built by another great disciple of Catherine, Blessed Giovanni Dominici, as part of an august altarpiece, now conserved in London, and the Dominican artist, Beato Angelico painted his sister with her head surrounded by supernatural rays. In Rome itself and in many other Italian cities and around the whole world, the cult of St. Catherine was eventually established, thanks to efforts of the artists who brought honour also upon themselves by offering their fairest flowers of homage. Upon the tomb of the great Pontiff Pius IX who ardently exalted her, there is a mosaic portrait of St. Catherine according to the design of "Lodovico Seit", as the protectress of the Papacy, in the act of holding up high the tiara and bringing it back to Rome. Thus all the plastic arts have offered their gracious homage to the great Saint whom Cornelius a Lapide called "the wonder of the world" almost as a humble token of love and gratitude for the incredible burst of enthusiasm with which she wholeheartedly embraced the Church and all humanity in one great act of faith and love.

WORKS OF AND ABOUT ST. CATHERINE
PUBLISHED BY EDIZIONI CANTAGALLI

SANTA CATERINA DA SIENA: IL DIALOGO DELLA DIVINA PROVVIDENZA, critical edition edited by GIULIANA CAVALLINI, pp. 658.

SANTA CATERINA DA SIENA: IL DIALOGO DELLA DIVINA PROVVIDENZA, edited by Tito Centi O.P., pp. 408.

SANTA CATERINA DA SIENA: LE ORAZIONI, edited by GIULIANA CAVALLINI, pp. 196.

SANTA CATERINA DA SIENA: LEGENDA MAIOR del Beato Raimondo da Capua, pp. 456.

LODOVICO FERRETTI: SANTA CATERINA DA SIENA, pp. 176 (available also in French, Spanish and German).

SANGUE E FUOCO. Florilegio dalle lettere di S. Caterina, edited by Mons. Antonio Bagnoli, pp. 192.

LETTERE SCELTE DI S. CATERINA DA SIENA, edited by Ambrogio Paganucci, pp. 312, paperback edition.

P. GIACINTO D'URSO, O.P.: SIA GRAZIA A TE. Meditazioni sulla spiritualità cateriniana, pp. 122.

GIOVANNI PAOLO II E ALTRI A.A.: IL SESTO CENTENARIO DEL TRANSITO DI S. CATERINA DA SIENA. Raccolta di scritti e discorsi pronunciati in occasione dell'anno centenario, pp. 88.

GIOVANNI PAOLO II: AMANTISSIMA PROVIDENTIA. Lettera apostolica nel VI centenario della morte di S. Caterina.

BRUNO ANCILLI: S. CATERINA DA SIENA VITA E OPERE, pp. 80.

S FRANCESCO E S. CATERINA PATRONI D'ITALIA, (Atti del Cinquantenario), pp. 96.

GABRIELLA ANODAL: IL LINGUAGGIO CATERINIANO. Indice delle immagini. Presentation by G. Cavallini, pp. XII/96.

P. GIACINTO D'URSO, O.P.: IL ROSARIO CON SANTA CATERINA, pp. 120.

CARLO RICCARDI: IL PENSIERO FILOSOFICO E MISTICO DI S. CATERINA DA SIENA, pp. 164.

CARLO RICCARDI: CATERINA DA SIENA E L'EUCARISTIA, pp. 240.

CARLO RICCARDI: BREVIARIO CATERINIANO, pp. 480.

CARLO RICCARDI: MARIA SANTISSIMA NELLA VITA E NEL PENSIERO DI S. CATERINA, pp. 112.

CARLO RICCARDI, IL MESSAGGIO DI S. CATERINA DA SIENA DOTTORE DELLA CHIESA, pp. 1212, hardcover edition with colour dust jacket.

...SCRIVO A VOI NEL PREZIOSO SANGUE SUO. S. Caterina parla ai giovani del terzo millenio, pp. 40.

PREGHIERE A S. CATERINA, pp. 32.

SANTA CATERINA DA SIENA - LEGENDA MINOR di Fra Tommaso da Siena detto il Caffarini, edited by Bruno Ancilli, pp. 224.

CON L'OCCHIO E COL LUME - (Atti del Corso Seminariale di Studi su S. Caterina da Siena. Siena October 1995), pp. 480.

P. ALFREDO ACARCIGLIA O.P.: S. CATERINA DIALOGA CON DIO PADRE MISERICORDIOSO, pp. 40.

LECTVRAE CATHARINE. S. Caterina da Siena e la pace, edited by the "Istituto Senese di Studi Cateriniani", Authors: Marco Bartoli, Antonio Volpato, Maria Grazia Bianco, Diega Giunta, pp. 80.

S. A TONIO PIEROZZI O.P.: STORIA BREVE DI S. CATERINA, TERZIARIA DOMENICANA, pp. 112.

UMBERTO MEATTINI: LETTERE DI S. CATERINA AGLI ER-
EMITANI DI LECCETO, illustrated, pp. 100.

Nelle librerie cattoliche o richieste direttamente a
EDIZIONI CANTAGALLI - Via Massetana Romana, 12
Casella Postale 155 - 53100 Siena - Tel. 0577 42102 Fax 0577 45363
e-mail: cantagalli@edizionicantagalli.com
www.edizionicantagalli.com